MEXICO CITY
AND
ACAPULCO

FODOR'S TRAVEL PUBLICATIONS

are compiled, researched, and edited by an international team of travel writers, field correspondents, and editors. The series, which now almost covers the globe, was founded by Eugene Fodor in 1936.

OFFICES
New York & London

Fodor's Mexico City and Acapulco:

Editor: Andrew E. Beresky
Area Editors: Jim Budd, Susan Wagner
Drawings: Edgar Blakeney
Maps: Marc Dinoir, Dyno Lowenstein

FODOR'S

MEXICO CITY
and
ACAPULCO
1988

FODOR'S TRAVEL PUBLICATIONS, INC.
New York & London

ISBN 0–679–01539–6
ISBN 0–340–41863–X (Hodder & Stoughton)

CONTENTS

Foreword

Mexico City and Acapulco vie with each other for the title as the most popular tourist destination south of the border. Each year, Mexico City attracts more than 2.6 million visitors, while Acapulco draws some 1.5 million sun worshippers to its white-sand beaches. While Mexico City successfully blends three cultures—pre-Columbian, Spanish, and modern—Acapulco primarily shimmers and glistens in the resort chic.

While every care has been taken to ensure the accuracy of the information contained in this guide, the publishers cannot accept responsibility for any errors which may appear.

All prices quoted in this guide are based on those available to us at the time of writing. In a world of rapid change, however, the possibility of inaccurate or out-of-date information can never be totally eliminated. We trust, therefore, that you will take prices quoted as indicators only, and will double-check to be sure of the latest figures.

Similarly, be sure to check all opening times of museums and galleries. We have found that such times are liable to change without notice, and you could easily make a trip only to find a locked door.

When a hotel closes or a restaurant produces a disappointing meal, let us know, and we will investigate the establishment and the complaint. We are always ready to revise our entries for the following year's edition should the facts warrant it.

Send your letters to the editors at Fodor's Travel Publications, 201 E. 50th Street, New York, NY 10022. European readers may prefer to write to Fodor's Travel Guides, 9–10 Market Place, London W1N 7AG, England.

FACTS AT YOUR FINGERTIPS

FACTS AT YOUR FINGERTIPS

INTRODUCTION. Mexico City and Acapulco offer much of Mexico's best: The dynamic, exciting capital is still Aztec, still viceregal Spanish, yet one of the world's great modern cities; the most glamorous Pacific port ranks as a premier resort in a country brimming with beaches. There was a time when everybody heading south of the border almost automatically opted for Mexico City and Acapulco. Now, there are other popular destinations, but both capital and Pacific port still serve as the best introduction to the magic of Mexico.

The areas surrounding these two cities also offer much to the traveler. Mexico City sits in the center of a fascinating region. There you can find the fabled pyramids of Teotihuacan; the stately, colonial city of Puebla; and the Indian market of Toluca. Acapulco's glitter and romance is enhanced by what may be the world's most beautiful bay, yet less than an hour away are great expanses of empty sand pounded by the Pacific surf as well as sleepy, palm-fringed lagoons all but untouched by the outside world. The road between the capital and the coast swings by Cuernavaca, hideaway for the rich, the famous, and the notorious. Beyond Cuernavaca lies Taxco nestled in hills. This centuries-old silver-mining town has been declared a national monument.

As you will see, the delights of Mexico City and Acapulco add up to unlimited fun, excitement, and adventure.

MEXICO CITY

Founded by the Aztecs in 1325, Mexico City is the oldest capital in the New World. It has also become the center of the largest metropolitan area on earth. According to some estimates, as many as eighteen million people live crowded into the Valley of Mexico at a breathtaking altitude of more than 7,000 feet.

The altitude accounts for a mild climate. Mexico City has an average year-round temperature of 60°F even though it is located in the tropics. The city can get either warm or cold but is rarely uncomfortable. It has a rainy season which runs roughly from May to October. During those months, the sun usually shines throughout the morning, but by late afternoon dark clouds gather to cover it; the rain, when it comes, falls in buckets.

One nice thing about the rain is that it washes away the smog. The lovely setting the Aztecs chose—a valley rimmed by tall mountains and snow-tipped volcanos in the east—is no longer "a region of most transparent air," as German traveler Alexander von Humbolt described it at the turn of the 19th century. Today that city on the lake is all too often under a pall of smoke and haze.

Almost as fascinating as the capital itself is the region that surrounds it. Puebla, one of North America's most Spanish cities, stands 80 miles to the east. Unlike Mexico City, which was built on the rubble of the Aztec's Tenochitlan, Puebla was built from scratch on a site where a bishop decreed a town should be built. Its contributions to the nation have included tile, onyx, and some of the finest dishes served from Mexican kitchens. Puebla claims its place in history as the site of the battle of the Cinco de Mayo (Fifth of May) where French troops were defeated in 1862. Just five miles from Puebla is Cholula, an archaeological site with a huge, still-buried pyramid and ruins of one of the holiest ancient cities.

Toluca, a provincial capital 40 miles west of Mexico City, hosts a well-known Indian market which is held on Fridays. The scenic highway leading there passes through cool pine forests.

1

South of Mexico's capital lies Cuernavaca, Taxco, and Acapulco.

ACAPULCO

Acapulco is still the biggest and, as many would say, the best of Mexico's world-class seaside resorts. It has everything from the sophisticated to the picturesque. Costera Boulevard, which hugs the city's beautiful bay, is grand, glamorous, and international. While "Traditional Acapulco," with its quaint hillside inns, exudes the full flavor of Mexico.

A wide range of choices for accommodations and entertainment also exist. You may want to relax in lavish bungalows with magnificent views, or opt for self-contained holiday hotels and never leave the grounds. You can golf at two of the finest courses in Mexico, play tennis after dark, and get up at dawn to go out on the sea in search of a sailfish. Or do what most people do—head for Acapulco for a wild and wonderful time.

PLANNING YOUR TRIP. Package tour or independent travel. Time, convenience, cost, and the type of travel that most interests you are the factors to consider when it comes to choosing an all-inclusive, fully escorted tour; a loose, plan-your-own-itinerary package tour; or totally independent travel. **Package tours** are the easiest to arrange and probably the most economical and efficient mode of travel for first-time visitors to Mexico, especially since most tourists want to divide their time between lying in the Acapulco sun and seeing the sights in Mexico City, and shopping, sampling the restaurants, and getting a taste of the nightlife. The operator will arrange for all plane, motorcoach, and other transportation, transfers wherever needed, tour guides, and generally commodious accommodations. Flight-plus-lodging with many such tours often works out to be less expensive than the flight alone as a regular economy fare. Thus, even if you prefer accommodations at someplace other than that offered by the tour operator (who usually has a selection of hotels to choose from according to the price-plan selected), and even if you have no intention of participating in any group sightseeing or other package activities, it may still be in your best interests to buy the entire package.

Among the general items to check when considering any package are these:

1. Does the price quoted cover air as well as land arrangements? If airfare is not included, does the tour operator have a special rate available?

2. How many meals are included?

3. How tied to the tour are you? If it is a motorcoach tour, for example, must you stay with the tour or can you leave and rejoin it at will?

4. Does the rate for an automobile included in the package carry an additional per-mile fee or is mileage unlimited? Is the car in the base rate exactly what you need? Air conditioning may or may not be necessary for you, but there is a substantial difference in charges for standard and automatic shifts. Driving a standard can save a great deal of money.

5. What is the tour operator's responsibility for getting you home on time (within reason, considering weather delays, etc.)?

In other words, read the fine print **very carefully.**

Traveling independently allows for greater freedom than group travel, but it is almost always more expensive for comparable accommodations and services. However, you will almost always get better value for your money (that does not necessarily mean it will be cheaper) when dining on your own, assuming you are not limiting your visit to a single resort hotel. Tour operators have arrangements with particular establishments that can handle busloads of tourists at a time; in order to serve them simultaneously and at a reduced rate, there will usually be a fixed menu offered or a limited selection from the full menu. The food in such places also tends to play on stereotypes; both your options and the quality of the food you get are likely to be better if you go it on your own.

If you have not tied yourself to a tour and do require assistance in finding accommodations within your budget, go directly to the information booths run by the Mexico City (Federal District) Tourism Office at the airport or at Calle Amberes between Londres and Hamburgo in the Pink Zone. This guide lists hotels in all price ranges. Acapulco has an information booth at the airport and on the highway just after entering the city, as well as booths and a tourist office on the Costera Boulevard.

In booking a package tour it is best to go through a travel agent; indeed, except for the likes of *American Express, Cook,* and the airlines, most packagers do not handle their own reservations.

TAKING MONEY ABROAD. Traveler's checks are still the standard and best way to safeguard your travel funds; and you will usually get a better exchange rate for them than for cash. In the U.S., many of the larger banks issue their own traveler's checks, which are just about as universally recognized as those of *American Express* and other top firms. In most instances there is a 1 percent charge for the checks; there is no fee for Barclays checks. Some banks also issue them free if you are a regular customer. The best-known British checks are those of *Cook* and *Barclays, Lloyds, Midland,* and *National Westminster* banks. It is also a good idea to have some local currency upon arrival. Some American banks will provide this service; alternatively, contact *Deak-Pererra,* 630 5th Ave., New York, NY 10036 (212–757–0100; call for additional branches). Major credit cards are accepted in Mexico in most large hotels, restaurants, and shops.

INSURANCE. The different varieties of travel insurance cover everything from health and accident costs to lost baggage to trip cancellation. Sometimes they can all be obtained with one blanket policy; sometimes they overlap with existing coverage you might have for health or home; and sometimes it is best to buy policies tailored to very specific needs. Insurance is available from numerous sources, and many travelers unwittingly end up with redundant coverage. Before purchasing separate travel insurance of any kind, be sure to check your regular policies carefully.

It is best to take care of your insurance needs before embarking on your trip. You'll pay more for less coverage—and have less chance to read the fine print— if you wait until the last minute and make your purchase from, say, an airport vending machine or insurance-company counter. If you have a regular insurance agent, he or she is the person to consult first.

Flight insurance, which is often included in the price of the ticket when the fare is paid via *American Express, Visa,* or certain other major credit cards, is also often included in package policies. Such policies, which provide accident coverage as well, are available from most tour operators and insurance companies. While it is a good idea to have health and accident insurance when traveling, be careful not to spend money to duplicate coverage you may already have. Then again, be careful not to neglect some eventuality which could end up costing a small fortune.

For example, basic *Blue Cross–Blue Shield* policies do cover health costs incurred while traveling. They will not, however, cover the cost of emergency transportation, which can often add up to several thousand dollars. Emergency transportation *is* covered, in part at least, by many major-medical policies, such as those underwritten by *Prudential, Metropolitan,* and *New York Life.* Again, we can't urge you too strongly to be sure you are getting the coverage you need and to check any policy carefully before buying. Another important example: Most insurance issued specifically for travel does not cover preexisting health conditions, such as a heart condition.

Several organizations offer coverage designed to supplement existing health insurance and help defray costs not covered by many standard policies, such as emergency transportation. Some of the more prominent are these:

NEAR (Nationwide Emergency Ambulance Return), 1900 N. McArthur Blvd., Suite 210, Oklahoma City, OK 73127 (800–654–6700). Rates range from $70 a person for 1–8 days, to $360 for a year.

Carefree Travel Insurance, c/o ARM Coverage, Inc., 9 E. 37th St., New York, NY 10016 (212–683–2622), offers medical evacuation arranged through Europe Assistance of Paris. Carefree's coverage is available from many travel agents.

International SOS Assistance, Inc., Box 11568, Philadelphia, PA 19116 (800–523–8930), has fees from $15 a person for 7 days to $195 for a year.

IAMAT (International Association for Medical Assistance to Travelers), 736 Center St., Lewiston, NY 14092 (716–754–4883) in the U.S.; or 188 Nicklin Road, Guelph, Ontario N1H 7L5 (519–836–0102) in Canada.

Another frequent inconvenience to travelers is loss of baggage. It is possible—though often it is a complicated affair—to insure your luggage against loss through theft or negligence. Insurance companies are reluctant to sell such coverage alone, however, since it is often a losing proposition for them. Instead, it is most often included as part of a package that would also cover accidents or health. Remuneration is often determined by weight, regardless of the value of the specific contents of the luggage. Insurance companies usually require documentation; should you lose your luggage or some other personal possession, be sure to report it to the local police immediately. Without documentation of such a report, your insurance company might be very stingy. Also, before buying baggage insurance, check your homeowners policy. Some such policies offer "off-premises theft" coverage, including loss of luggage while traveling.

The last major area of traveler's insurance is trip cancellation coverage. This is especially important to travelers on APEX or charter flights. Should you get sick abroad, or for some other reason be unable to continue your trip, you may be stuck having to buy a new one-way fare home, plus pay for space on the charter you're not using. You can guard against this with trip cancellation insurance, usually available from travel agents. Most of these policies will also cover last-minute cancellations.

HOW TO GET THERE. By Air: Air fares are in a constant state of flux, and our best advice is to have your reservations made by a travel agent. Agents are familiar with the latest changes in fare structures—ever more confusing despite "deregulation" among U.S. carriers, who now allegedly base prices on distance traveled—as well as with the rules governing various discount plans. Among those rules are: booking (usually) 21–30 days in advance, minimum stay requirements, maximum stay allowances, a payment in advance (sometimes) for land arrangements. Lowest prices overall will, of course, be during the off-season.

Generally, on regularly scheduled flights, you have the option, in descending order of cost, of First Class, Club or Business Class, Economy, or APEX. APEX is by far the most used and the most useful of these categories. Some charter service is still available; again, an agent will be able to recommend which ones are reliable. Sometimes it is also worth investigating package tours for flights even if you do not wish to use a tour's other services (hotels, meals, etc.). Because a packager can block-book seats, the price of a flight-plus-lodging package can actually be less than the cost of air fare that is booked separately.

If you have the flexibility, you can sometimes benefit from last-minute sales which tour operators have in order to fill a plane or bus. A number of brokers specializing in such discount sales have also sprung up. All charge an annual membership fee, usually about $35–$45. Among these are *Stand-Buys Ltd.,* Box 2088, Southfield, MI 48037 (800–621–5839); *Moments Notice,* 40 E. 49th St., New York, NY 10017 (212–486–0503); *Discount Travel Intl.,* 114 Forrest Ave., Narbeth, PA 19072 (800–458–5200); and *Worldwide Discount Travel Club,* 1674 Meridian Ave., Miami Beach, FL 33139 (305–895–2082). Sometimes tour and charter-flight operators themselves advertise in Sunday travel supplements, as well. Do try to find out whether the tour operator is reputable, and, specifically, whether you are tied to a precise round trip or whether you will have to wait until the operator has a spare seat in order to return.

Airlines specifically serving Mexico City and Acapulco from major U.S. cities include: *Aeroméxico,* 8390 NW 53rd St., Miami FL 33166 (305–592–1300) flies nonstop to Mexico City from Miami, New York, and Houston; to Acapulco nonstop from Houston daily, New York twice weekly, and Toronto once a week. *Mexicana,* 9841 Airport Blvd., Los Angeles CA 90045 (800–421–2214) flies to Mexico City nonstop from Los Angeles, San Antonio, Chicago, and Dallas; to Acapulco from Los Angeles and Dallas. *Pan Am,* Pan Am Building, New York, NY 10017 (212–687–2600) comes in daily nonstop from Washington. *Continental,* 2929 Allen Pkwy., Houston, TX 77210 flies nonstops from Atlanta, New York and Houston to both Mexico City and Acapulco. *Western,* 6060 Avion Dr., Los Angeles, CA 90009 (213–636–2345), flies nonstops from Los Angeles to both Mexico City and Acapulco. *American Airlines,* Dallas–Fort Worth Airport, Dallas, TX 75261 (817–355–1234) has two nonstop flights from both Chicago and Dallas: one to Mexico City and one to Acapulco. *Braniff* flies non-stop to Mexico City from San Antonio and Dallas–Fort Worth with service to Acapulco during the winter months.

From Canada: *Aeromexico,* 85 Richmond St., Toronto (800–AEROMEX) flies from Toronto once a week via Acapulco.

Typical fares as of mid-1986:

New York to Mexico City, $400–$420 excursion depending on season. Dallas to Mexico City, $275 round-trip excursion. Charter fares are about the same as, or slightly lower than, excursion.

From Britain: *British Airways,* Heathrow Airport, London, (01–759–5511) connects daily with Mexicana in Chicago for one-stop service.

Air France, 158 New Bond St., London W1 (01–499–9511), flies to Mexico City via Paris and New York, and can arrange onward flights within Mexico.

Iberia, 169 Regent St., London W1 (01–437–5622), flies to Mexico City three to four times a week from Madrid. They have two flights daily from London to Madrid.

K.L.M., Time and Life Building, New Bond Street, London W1 (01–568–9144), flies to Mexico City most days of the week, via Amsterdam, and will arrange onward internal flights if requested.

Typical fares as of mid-1985:

London to Mexico City, £1,000 Economy year-round, no restrictions; £576 PEX/Budget low season, restrictions on length of stay, etc.; £633 PEX/Budget high season, restrictions on length of stay.

By Sea: Cruises. Many cruises include Acapulco as part of their itinerary. Most originate from Los Angeles.

Empress Travel's cruise packages to Acapulco and Mexico City feature choice of hotel and round trip via Aeromexico from New York. Cruises leave from San Francisco.

Cruise operators you may wish to contact (though bookings are generally handled through a travel agent): *Sundance Cruises,* Suite 2200, 520 Pike St., Seattle, WA 98901 (800–222–5505); *Sitmar Cruises,* 10100 Santa Monica Blvd., Los Angeles, CA 90067 (800–421–0880); *Holland American Lines,* 300 Elliott Ave. W., Seattle, WA 98119 (800–426–0327); *Carnival Cruise Lines,* 5225 NW 87th Ave., Miami, FL 33166 (305–599–2600); *Princess Cruises,* 2029 Century Park East, Los Angeles, CA 90067 (213–553–1770); *Royal Viking Line,* One Embarcadero Center, San Francisco, CA 94111 (800–422–8000).

For details on the possibility of freighter travel to or from Mexico, consult either of the following specialists: *Air Marine Travel Service,* 501 Madison Ave., New York, NY 10022, publisher of the *Trip Log Quick Reference Freighter Guide;* or *Pearl's Freighter Tips,* 175 Great Neck Rd., Great Neck, NY 11021.

Bus or Rail: Bus or rail travel to Mexico City involves a transfer at one of the Texas border cities such as El Paso, Laredo, or Brownsville to board a Mexican bus. Bus travel in Mexico is quite inexpensive and the first class and deluxe service is fairly good. As for rail lines, the *Regiomontano,* with sleepers, dining and club car, leaves Nuevo Laredo (across from Laredo Texas) daily for Mexico City. *Amtrak's* train from Chicago requires an overnight stay in Laredo. For rail connections to the *National Railways of Mexico,* U.S. passenger representatives are located at 1100 17th St. NW, Suite 907, Washington, DC 20036 (202–347–4518/19); and 1500 Broadway, New York, NY 10036 (212–382–2262).

GETTING AROUND BY CAR. An automobile is almost useless in big, confusing Mexico City, but more than handy in Acapulco. For anyone with the time—two or three weeks—driving to Mexico City and on to Acapulco can be a memorable adventure.

Whether those memories are fond ones, however, depends on many factors, including good luck. Bear in mind that Mexico is part of the Third World, a far cry from the rest of North America or Western Europe.

The biggest problem at this writing is finding unleaded gasoline. Since the September 1985 earthquakes, promises have been made to correct the situation, but drivers should check with an auto club to find out if the promises have been kept.

Spare parts are another worry. Only cars made in Mexico are sold in Mexico. Parts for these vehicles are plentiful, but getting a gizmo for a Toyota or Mercedes is not easy.

The best highway, although two lanes most of the way, is #85 from Laredo to Monterrey and #57 on to Mexico City. Driving time is about 16 hours.

The trip to Acapulco from Mexico City takes about six hours, but many people opt for going via Taxco and spending at least one night there.

Practical tips to drivers. There are two absolutely essential things to remember about driving in Mexico. First and foremost is to carry insurance. If you injure anyone in an accident, you could well be jailed—whether it was your fault or not—unless you have insurance. This is part of the country's *Code Napoléon:* guilty until proven innocent.

The second item is that if you enter Mexico with a car, you must leave with it. The fact that you drove in with a car is stamped on your tourist card, which you must give to immigration authorities at departure. If an emergency arises and you must fly home, there are complicated procedures to face with customs. The reason is that cars are much cheaper in the U.S., and you are not allowed to sell your vehicle in Mexico. The authorities at the airport assume that, unless you have a customs release, you have sold your car for a hefty profit. Explaining that your beloved mother-in-law is in the hospital or that your business is about to collapse cuts no ice. If such a situation should arise, contact the customs officials at the airport to see if you may leave your car in their special parking lot.

Mileage and speed limits are given in kilometers; 100 kph and 80 kph (62 and 50 miles, respectively) are the most common maximum speeds. A few of the newer toll roads allow 110 kph (approx. 68.4 mph). Cities and towns may have posted speed limits of 40 kph (25 miles), sometimes even 30 kph (18 miles), and it's best to observe them. To convert kilometers to miles, multiply by .62, or get a rough idea by remembering that 100 kilometers is about 60 miles.

The one-way street is widely used in most communities through which you may drive. Your guide is an arrow posted on the sides of corner buildings, its point indicating the direction of traffic flow. A two-pointed arrow means two-way traffic. The arrow may have the words *tránsito* or *circulación* printed on it.

In town a sign with a large *E* inside a circle stands for *estacionamiento,* or parking. Much more frequently seen is the same sign with a strong bar diagonally through the *E* and maybe the word *NO* underneath—no parking!

When you approach a narrow bridge *(puente angosto)* at the same time another car approaches the opposite end, the first one to flick his lights has the right of way.

Don't drive at night unless absolutely necessary, and even then only on the superhighways. The hazards are too many—you can't see perambulating animals soon enough; large rocks may have been left on the pavement by some motorist who had car trouble and braced his wheels with them, and then unthinkingly drove off without removing them; a pedestrian or cyclist appears around a sudden curve; new rock slides occur in mountain areas during the rainy season; potholes abound—the list is a long one and the risk not worth the little mileage gained.

During the day be alert to cattle crossings. Free-grazing animals may decide to amble across the highway just as you approach. Domestic animals frequently graze along the shoulders and the sight or sound of an approaching car could cause one or more to bolt—not always away from the pavement. Advises a Mexican, "An older animal is wise to the dangers of the highway and will seldom move fast, but watch for the young ones, like calves. They're nervous and easily frightened into bolting."

There are several toll roads in Mexico, covering mostly the last stretches of major highways leading to the capital. Some of these roads are two-lane affairs but most are four-lane with a divider strip. These highways have non-toll roads running roughly parallel. The toll roads have signs that say *cuota* and give the destination (usually *Mexico,* meaning Mexico City and perhaps an intermediary city) while the parallel routes have signs saying *libre* (free) with the destination. These two signs, with arrows pointing in different directions, are usually posted before the road splits. Remember that because of the mountainous nature of central and southern Mexico and the many trucks on the highways, driving times are longer than for comparable distances in the U.S. There are also toll bridges in various parts of the country.

When you buy insurance, you will probably receive a folder showing Mexican road signs. The essential markers are obvious even if your Spanish is nonexistent. *No* means no, and arrows show what's forbidden. Take a good look at the sign diagrams and keep them handy until you have them memorized. Here are a few words on the road signs that you should know: *alto*—stop; *no rebase*—do not pass; *ceda el paso*—yield right of way; *conserva su derecha*—keep to the right; *curva peligrosa*—dangerous curve; *derrumbes*—landslide zone; *despacio* (sometimes also *disminuye su velocidad*)—slow down; *tramo en reparacion*—road work ahead; *puente angosto*—narrow bridge; *no hay paso*—road closed; *desviacion*—detour.

Topes, meaning bumps, are indicated by a sign showing a series of bumps. As many highways—sometimes even major ones—cut through towns and villages, these bumps are the only way to slow down the speeding traffic to protect life and livestock. At times the bumps are so worn down that you don't even have to slow down, but elsewhere you have to come to an almost complete halt to make it over without damage to your vehicle, especially if it is low slung. Best to slow down when approaching any village—at times the bumps are there but the signs are not.

If an oncoming vehicle flicks its lights at you during daytime, it could mean trouble ahead. Best to slow down for a while and see what's around the curves, so that you won't run into a landslide, a stalled truck, or an accident.

As you climb into the highlands of central Mexico, your car might not feel quite right due to the altitude. This could be a result of the lower octane gasoline or your carburetor's needing adjustment.

Road maps are handy for those travelling by car in Mexico. A large selection of the most up-to-date maps are available from Bradt Enterprises, 95 Harvey St., Cambridge, MA 02140.

Aid to Motorists: The "Green Angels." The Mexican Tourism Secretariat operates a fleet of more than 227 special pickup trucks on all the nation's major highways to render assistance to motorists. Known officially as the *Tourist Assistance Service,* one and all, familiarly and with affection, call them the *Green Angels.* The billingual drivers are equipped to offer mechanical first aid to your car, medical first aid to you, communication through a two-way radio-telephone network, basic supplies of all types, towing if needed, adjustment and changing of tires, tourist information, and protection. The trucks are painted two shades of green and have a flashing red light atop the cab. The doors carry printed identification in English and Spanish. The number of Green Angels has been increased in recent years.

How to hail one in case of need? Pull off the road as far as possible and lift the hood of your car. If on an isolated section of highway, then hail the first passing car in either direction and ask the driver to notify the patrol of your trouble. Bus drivers and drivers of heavy trucks will also be helpful in this respect.

The patrol's services are rendered free of charge. Tips, however, are not refused. Any spare parts, fuel, or lubricants they supply to get your car back on the road are provided at cost.

The Green Angels patrol fixed sections of highway, passing a given spot several times a day. The service is provided from 8 A.M. to around 8 P.M. every day on major highways. But remember, this is Mexico, not Switzerland. Most likely, a Green Angel will come along if you have mechanical problems, but you can't always count on it.

Insurance. Remember that your foreign car insurance coverage is not good in Mexico. Purchase enough Mexican automobile insurance at the border to cover your estimated trip. It's sold by the day, and if your trip is shorter than your original estimate, a prorated refund for the unused time will be issued to you upon application after you exit the country. *Dan Sanborn's Insurance* and *Seguros Atlantico* (Allstate reps) have offices in most border cities. Also, you might try *Instant Mexico Auto Insurance,* San Ysidro and Chula Vista, CA, and Nogales, AZ. All three are experienced, reliable.

Always lock your car securely in Mexico when no one's in it. *Never* leave valuable items in the body of the car; either lock them in the truck compartment or carry them into your hotel or motel with you at night.

At a service station. Your American gasoline charge cards won't work in Mexico. All service stations are *Pemex*—the national gas company. Stations are fairly few and far between. Always fill up once the guage hits the half-empty mark.

Regular gasoline, around 80 octane, was selling for 75 U.S. cents a gallon at press time. Regular gas is sold out of blue pumps. When available, nonleaded Extra, around 90 octane, is sold out of silver-colored pumps. It was going for 120 pesos a liter or roughly 95 cents a gallon. (The red pumps are for diesel fuel.)

Pumps measure gas not by the gallon, but by the liter. A liquid liter is 1.057 quarts; 3.784 liters equals 1 gallon.

Oil: Pemex's *Faja de Oro* (black and gold can), *Esso, Shell, Quaker State,* and *Mobiloil* are best grades of motor oil. Pemex products usually cost less. Mexican-made tires are of good quality but more expensive than in the U.S. and Canada.

Restrooms have undergone modernizing, too, and are periodically inspected for cleanliness and serviceability. In between inspections, however, some station operators neglect them, while others, to assure their proper maintenance, keep them under lock and key. If you must ask for the key to a locked restroom, for women it's *"la llave para damas, por favor"* (lah yah-vay pah-rah dah-mahs, pohr fah-vohr); for men, *"caballeros"* (cah-bah-YEHR-ohs).

Tell the attendant *"Lleno, por favor"* (YAY-noh)—that is, "Fill'er up." Point out the pump you want. Most cars do well on the *Nova* (blue pump), but if yours is a late U.S. model you'll need the *Extra* (nonleaded, in silver pump). Check to be sure the pump gauge is turned back to zero before the attendant starts pumping your gas; as soon as the tank is filled write down the amount of pesos shown as due. In a busy station—and most highway stations are—a second attendant may turn the gauge back to zero to service another car and your amount due may be forgotten (or escalated). Write it down to be on the safe side.

Attendants don't jump to clean your windshield the moment you pull in. As a general rule you must ask to have this done. Also, you may have to ask for under-the-hood inspection and checking of tire pressure. A tip, the equivalent of a dime or a quarter for these extra services is customary and expected. The gas stations do not have mechanics.

Automobile repair. You may have heard tales about how Mexican mechanics put motors back together with bobby pins and glue. True, the mechanics are resourceful and capable, as evidenced by the large numbers of vintage automobiles still daily plying the streets. Finding U.S.-made spare parts can be a major problem—so is trying to locate an English-speaking mechanic. We suggest that you ask for help at your hotel if you need mechanical work done on your car.

Parking. We suggest parking in pay lots, usually called *estacionamiento* (parking), as towing away illegally parked cars is becoming common.

Those missing license plates. Mexican police have always employed a most effective means for punishing those who park their automobiles in forbidden areas—they remove one license plate. Redeeming it requires a trip to the local *tránsito* headquarters and the payment of a fine.

Witnessing an accident. When you see an accident or an injured person, don't stop to help. Instead, notify the first policeman you see or, if on the highway, the first Green Angel Tourism Secretariat truck or highway patrol car. Not helping personally is against one's instincts and training, but it can get you seriously involved, even thrown in jail. You can be accused of *mal medicina,* for instance, if you move an injured person. He, or the police, can later charge you made things worse for him, or, in the extreme, if he dies you could be accused of causing it. Far better to locate the nearest official and *then* offer your help.

Police. The color and cut of police uniforms vary throughout the Mexican Republic. Mexico City traffic and civil police all wear blue uniforms—with the addition of white gloves for dress occasions. Other special police units in the capital: park police (including young women), navy blue and grey; parking police, khaki; bank and other guards, navy blue. The city fathers have striven to assign bilingual officers along downtown to better offer directions and any other assistance to tourists.

Fly and drive. Not much vacation time? Fly to Mexico City or Acapulco and rent an automobile to get around in. Your travel agent can make advance reservations, and your car will be waiting for you at the airport of arrival.

Another suggestion: Make the fullest use of your available time and see more of the countryside by alternating flying and driving to various key cities, always making advance reservations to avoid possible delay. The larger auto rental firms in Mexico publish folders in English outlining such suggested Fly-Drive Tours.

The most popular rental cars in Mexico have been Volkswagen sedans and combis, Nissan sedans and station wagons, Dodge Dart, Volare, Caribe, Gremlin, Rambler, Malibu, and Caprice; for larger models, Chrysler's Le Baron and Ford's LTD.

Rental cars are expensive in Mexico. Daily rates average $50 with insurance and taxes, plus some 15 cents (U.S.) per kilometer. Weekly rates at the time of this writing were between $350 and $400, with unlimited mileage and including insurance and taxes. These rates are for the smallest model cars such as the VW Beetle. Larger models are proportionately higher. As some companies run promotions at various times, it might save you some money to check and compare prices. During busy holiday periods, reserve your car ahead of time.

Requirements: over 24 years of age, valid driver's license, passport or tourist card, and a major credit card.

The central reservations numbers in Mexico City for major companies are given below. Most of the auto rental firms have service stands at the international airport, as well as several outlets in the capital and in Acapulco.

Avis, tel: 578–1044; *Budget,* tel: 566–6800; *Hertz,* tel: 566–0099; *National Car Rental,* tel: 533–0375; *Ford Rente,* tel: 564–7834; *Romano Rent-a-Car,* tel: 250–0055 and 545–5722; *Quick Rent-a-Car,* tel: 533–4908 and 533–5335.

PASSPORTS. Passports are not formally required for entry into Mexico by U.S. citizens, though some proof of citizenship is. Also suitable is a birth certificate or voter registration card, plus tourist card. The latter can be obtained from a travel agent or an airline agent at the airport or from local Mexican consulates.

Canadian citizens need only their provincial birth certificate and tourist card. Again, the latter is available from travel agents and airlines.

British subjects need a valid passport and a Mexican tourist card. Passport may be secured from the Passport Office, London, from passport offices in Glasgow, Liverpool, Newport, and Peterborough, or from any British consulate abroad. It is valid for ten years. Mexican tourist card may be secured from the Mexican Embassy, 8 Halkin St., London S.W.1, or the Tourist Office, 7 Cork St., London W.1; or, if already abroad, from any Mexican embassy and national airlines. Students wishing to study in Mexico and business travelers must inquire at the consulate for additional requirements. Passport or other proof of citizenship must be presented to re-enter Great Britain. No limit on amount of money carried out of the country for pleasure travel.

TRAVEL AGENTS. The critical issues in choosing a travel agent are how knowledgeable that person is about travel and how reliable his or her bookings are, regardless of whether you are looking for a package tour or planning to go it independently. The cost will be substantially the same whether you go to a major tour operator such as *Maupintour, American Express, Thos. Cook & Son,* or *Olson's* or to the small agency around the corner. Most commissions are paid by airlines, hotels, and tour operators. In Europe there may be a small general service charge or fee-per-reservation; in the U.S. only out-of-the-ordinary telephone or telex charges are ever paid by the client.

The importance of a travel agent is not merely for making reservations, however. A good travel agent booking a flight for you will know what general discounts are in effect based on how long your stay will be, how far in advance you are able to make your reservations, whether you are making a simple round trip or adding extra stops, and other factors. He or she will also likely be able to suggest suitable accommodations or packages that offer the kind of services you want.

In the case of package tours, you want to be sure that the tour operator can deliver the package being offered. Here again, a travel agent can be helpful. Certainly the organizations named above have established their reputations based on reliability—the inevitable occasional foul-up notwithstanding.

Not all U.S. travel agents are licensed, as the laws vary from state to state, but membership in the American Society of Travel Agents (ASTA) is a safeguard. Similarly, U.K. agents belong to the Association of British Travel Agents (ABTA). Members prominently display ASTA or ABTA shields.

TOUR OPERATORS. In addition to airlines, cruise lines and hotel chains, a number of tour operators—known in the trade as "wholesalers"—offer a variety of package programs to either or both Mexico City and Acapulco. In most cases these call for independent travel, although groups are handled as well. A typical package includes air transportation, airport transfers, hotels, and sightseeing. Many feature land transportation one way to Acapulco with a night in Taxco. These operators generally market their packages only through retail travel agents, but since not all retailers handle all tour operators, you might wish to contact the various organizations to learn what they have available.

American Express, 822 Lexington Ave., New York, NY 10021 (800–241–1700).

American Leisure, 9800 Centre Parkway, Houston, TX 77036 (800–231–5804).

Cartan Travel, One Crossroads of Commerce, Rolling Meadows, IL 60008 (800–323–7888).

Compass Tours, 330 Seventh Ave., New York, NY 10001 (212–714–0200).

Four Winds Travel, 175 Fifth Ave., New York, NY 10010 (212–777–0260).

GoGo Travel, 432 Park Ave. South, New York, NY 10016 (212–683–7744).

Asti Tours, 21 E. 40th St., New York, NY 10016 (800–223–7728).

Betanzos Tours, 323 Geary St., San Francisco, CA 94930 (415–421–0955).

Club Universe, 1671 Wilshire Blvd., Los Angeles, CA 90017 (800–252–0862).

Friendly Holidays, 118–21 Queens Blvd., Forest Hills, NY 11375 (800–221–9748).

Garza Tours, 14103 Riverside Dr., Sherman Oaks, CA 91423 (800–423–3178).

Intersol, 8939 Sepulvada Blvd., Los Angeles, CA 90045 (800–421–5365).

Mexico Travel Advisors, 1717 N. Highland Ave., Los Angeles, CA 90028 (800–421–4037).

Thompson Vacations, 401 N. Michigan Ave., Chicago, IL 60611 (800–621–6400).

 TOURIST INFORMATION SERVICES. The major source of information for anyone planning a vacation to Mexico City or Acapulco is the *Mexican Government Tourist Office,* 405 Park Ave., New York, NY 10022, 212–755–7212. They can supply information on all aspects of travel, from which type of vacation is best suited to your needs and purse, to the best and most economical ways of satisfying your goals. They will also have a wealth of material on hotels, restaurants, excursions, museums, and so on. They produce copious amounts of information, much of it free and all of it useful.

Mexico City. The *Federal District Tourist Office* is at the corner of Amberes and Londres in the Pink Zone, with branches at the airport and at bus depots. Information is available by phone, 525–9380, from 9 A.M to 9 P.M.

Acapulco. The state tourist office is at Costera Blvd. 54, across from the CiCi Park, tel. 4–6134.

MEETING THE MEXICANS. The best way to get the feel of a country is to spend some time with its native inhabitants, learning their ways and native customs. In Mexico, for example, formality and tradition are very important. Yet Mexicans are easygoing and relaxed, and the notion of things moving rather slowly down there is not a stereotype.

Some organizations in Mexico City that can help you get to know your hosts: *Mexican-North American Cultural Institute,* Hamburgo 115, tel. 511–4720; *Anglo-Mexican Cultural Institute,* Antonio Caso 127, tel. 566–4500; *University Club,* Reforma 150, tel. 566–2266. Arrange for a guest card through your hotel.

TIPS FOR BRITISH VISITORS. National Tourist Office. 7 Cork St., London W1 (tel. 01–734 1058/9). **Insurance.** We heartily recommend that you insure yourself to cover health and motoring mishaps, with *Europ Assistance,* 252 High St., Croydon CRO 1NF (tel. 01–680 1234). When you need help, there is a 24-hour, seven days a week (all holidays included) telephone service staffed by multilingual personnel.

Money Matters. It is best to provide yourself with U.S. traveler's checks or dollar bills, as they are much easier to change than European currencies.

Electricity. Usually 110 volts. You should take along an adaptor, as razor and hair-dryer sockets are usually of the American style, taking flat-pronged plugs.

Tour Operators. *Bales Tours,* Bales House, Barrington Rd., Dorking, Surrey RH4 3EJ (tel. 0306–885991), offer a 15-day escorted tour "The Aztecs and Mayas" for £1,180. This tour looks at the archaeological sites in the mountains of Central Mexico and the jungles of the Yucatan. *Kuoni Travel,* 33 Maddox St., London W1 (tel. 01–499 8636) has a "Mexican Panorama" tour to Mexico City, Merida, Oaxaca, and Acapulco; 12 nights from £1,154. They also offer 12 nights in a luxury resort hotel in Acapulco, starting at £1,165.

Swan Hellenic, Canberra House, 47 Middlesex St., London E1 (tel. 01–247 0401) offers a 17-day tour looking at the art treasures of Mexico, accompanied by a tour manager and a guest lecturer. £1,785.

 WHEN TO GO. Unlike resort areas, Mexico City has no official high and low season with corresponding differences in hotel rates. Weather, however, is more pleasant during the winter months and is rather like autumn in New York. May or June into October tends to be rainy and sometimes a bit chilly. Holy Week (just before Easter) and Christmas Week (just before New Year's) are when *capitalinos* head for the beaches, leaving Mexico City with fewer crowds, little traffic, and almost no smog.

In Acapulco the high season is from December 15 through Holy Week (when it is jammed). The rest of the year prices dip by at least one-third. Early spring and late fall are the best times to take advantage of bargain rates. Summer is the rainy season and there are times when it rains for days on end. Even when it does not rain, Acapulco can be muggy in summer (and full of vacationing Mexican families with their children in the pools).

 MONEY. The peso has been steadily losing value in relation to other currencies, often by as much as 10% or 15% a month. Traveler's checks and dollars are easy to exchange for pesos. Rates, however, vary slightly from place to place: Exchange houses *(casas de cambio)*—which are found in all tourist areas—pay a bit more for dollars than banks; hotels pay the least. Best bet is to change no more money than is necessary, using credit cards wherever possible (one loses changing pesos back to dollars). With the peso falling but inflation over 100%, prices listed in these pages may be somewhat out of date by the time you arrive.

Most major U.S. credit cards are accepted in Mexico City and Acapulco—in the better hotels and restaurants—but as policies change, it is advisable to check before planning a credit card splurge. In smaller towns and rural areas, forget about using credit cards unless at a foreign tourist-oriented hotel or restaurant.

Traveler's checks are widely accepted. Banks usually provide the best rate of exchange, but you might lose time if things are busy. Most airports have money exchanges at the same rate as banks. You can usually get more pesos for your dollars at Mexican airports or banks than at U.S. airports, which often charge a 1% commission.

We advise that you change your traveler's checks gradually, as you need them, throughout your vacation. This will protect you in case of theft and you will receive a bit more for your dollars the longer you wait, due to the gradual slide (devaluation). Although it is not advisable to keep large amounts of cash on you, private money exchangers in resorts or the big cities can give you 10 to 20 pesos more to the dollar (cash only) than the banks.

 WHAT TO TAKE. Every guidebook ever published has set forth the same advice to anyone contemplating a foreign trip: *travel light!* And every tourist always takes too much anyway.

If traveling by air to Mexico, you are limited to 2 bags not to exceed 132 lbs. Of course, if you are driving your own automobile, you have greater flexibility. Yet it is never wise to burden yourself with more than you, one person, can comfortably carry.

For air travel two average-size suitcases, or one spacious suitcase and one fold-over garment bag, should be sufficient and should come within the allowable weight limits. The suitcases should preferably be of the flexible, lightweight types especially manufactured for air travel.

When coming to Mexico by plane, we recommend your two suitcases be packed very lightly, enabling you later on to put the bulk of your clothing into one and your purchases into the other. (Carry-on cases or bags are presumably limited to a size that will fit under your seat, and some carriers are strict about enforcing this.) If driving, it's not a bad idea to bring one entirely empty suitcase or other sturdy container for the same purpose—to hold all your purchases.

What to bring to wear. Acapulco is a casually elegant playground. No jackets or ties for men; nothing that will wilt for ladies. Unless you have a well-stocked resort wardrobe, it is better to pack light and buy on arrival. Acapulco is noted for its high-style vacation wear.

Mexico City is, and has always been, both dressy and conservative-minded. Here women will need a small supply of street dresses—all those marvelous new fabrics that are drip-dry, wrinkleproof, and so on—plus one lightweight wool suit, a sweater or two, at least two simple cocktail dresses or dressy pantsuits. In the winter, an all-weather coat and perhaps something to protect the head (Mexican rebozos do beautifully here!). Always, at least one pair of dress shoes, one or two pairs of comfortable, well-broken-in walking shoes; other shoes as desired, or as packing space allows.

Until recently women were warned of Mexico City's extreme conservatism—no wearing of shorts, slacks, nothing way-out in the way of personal street wear. This is no longer entirely true. Mexican women have adopted pantsuits for day and evening wear with great enthusiasm, hence their visiting counterparts should be allowed the same latitude. Keep current styles in mind when preparing to come to Mexico's capital. The city has become very fashion conscious in recent years. Strangely, the familiar warning against either men or women wearing ordinary walking shorts on Mexico City streets is still valid.

Normally, formal wear will not be needed, unless you may be invited to a dressy diplomatic affair. A light wrap, if not too bulky, may come in handy for chilly evenings. But why not save precious packing space and buy a pretty Mexican *rebozo* (shawl) after arrival.

Men will need one dark suit, with appropriate accessories, for dress. Otherwise, a plentiful supply of slacks, one or two sport jackets, sport shirts, one or two long-sleeved, drip-dry shirts, a sweater or two, and at least one pair of sandals, tennis shoes, or comfortable walking shoes. During the winter, a light topcoat. During the summer: a raincoat or light all-weather coat that can serve in rain, as well as some type of cap. One or two ties—some city restaurants will not admit a man without jacket and tie. Men will want to buy at least one *Guayabera* shirt while in Mexico. Called the most practical men's shirt ever invented, it is worn outside the trousers.

Except for visiting country Indians who always wear them, neither men nor women wear hats in Mexico City as a general rule. It is no longer a requirement for women to cover their heads when entering a church or cathedral, but many still feel more at ease with a handkerchief or light scarf over their hair.

Both men and women: A pair of tennis shoes or other sturdy, rubber-soled footgear is a necessity if you plan to go pyramid climbing, or if a visit to the cobblestone-streeted cities of Taxco is included in your itinerary. The centuries-old pyramid steps and cobblestones are well worn and slippery under leather soles.

Precaution for automobile travel: If you are getting around via car with a guide-driver, one of the first things he will tell you is not to leave any of your possessions in sight in the body of the car when you are not occupying it. This means, when sightseeing or shopping during the day, lock everything in the car trunk.

The warning is even more important when you are driving your own automobile, that is, one with foreign license plates. Discourage thievery by taking anything expensive—camera, tape recorder, radio, and the like—into your motel or hotel room at night. Keep your luggage locked when you are out of your room. Try not to park your car overnight on the street—most hotels have garages or parking lots with night guards—and always lock your car unless you need to leave your key with the parking attendant. These simple precautions have become a modern necessity almost anywhere in the world, and Mexico is no exception.

Other helpful items to bring: Your camera, of course. No country is more photogenic than Mexico. Each person is allowed to bring in one regular and one movie camera, with 12 rolls of film for each, and it's a good idea to bring the limit because you might not find your favorite make of film. Your citizens band radio is now allowed free entry. A small flashlight will prove its value many times over—the electric power sometimes goes on and off like a yo-yo.

Bring at least one can of spray insect repellant with you. Bugs are not very troublesome either in Mexico City or Acapulco, but it is best to be prepared.

Also, among smaller items: tweezers, small scissors, a roll of cellophane or magic transparent tape, a few rubber bands, a notebook or two and ballpoint pens, and a sewing kit that includes a few spare buttons. A plentiful supply of paper tissues or a roll of toilet tissue, a bar of soap in a small plastic container, and maybe a small quantity of paper towels. As in so many parts of the world, public restrooms in Mexico often lack these items. A small-size plastic bottle or other container of your favorite powdered detergent—avoid liquids if possible. Cream or powder perfumes and colognes are preferable to the liquid; if you do bring the liquid variety, be sure to seal the top with cellophane.

●

WHAT IT WILL COST. Going all out and spending freely, the budget for a day in Acapulco might be as follows:

Double room with taxes	$125
Meals for two with moderate drinking	105
Drinks and show at a nightclub	55
Cocktails	15
Tips	20
	$320

This is the big splurge. You can easily cut costs in half by staying in a less expensive hotel, and eating at a less expensive restaurant. In Mexico City, you can easily lop off 30% from the above prices. The main items in your budget will be hotels and restaurants, covered below. In general, the more Spanish you speak, the cheaper it will be to travel, especially if you are willing to risk eating Mexican cuisine and going without confirmed reservations.

 SEASONAL EVENTS. Every day is a fiesta day somewhere in Mexico. In the capital or Acapulco you are fairly likely to bump into one celebration or another.

January 1—New Year's Day, a quiet holiday after the big night before. As many vacationers return home Jan. 1, it is a good day to avoid travel.

January 6—Three Kings Day (Santos Keyes), observed all over Mexico. This is the traditional date when Mexican children set out their shoes, expecting them to be filled with gifts.

January 17—San Antonio Abad and Blessing of the Animals. All over Mexico not only household pets, but cows, pigs, and chickens, all flower- and ribbon-bedecked, are carried or led to the churches for priestly blessing.

January 18—Santa Prisca, in Taxco, state of Guerrero; fiesta of the silver town's patroness.

February-March—Pre-Lenten Carnaval celebrated in Tepoztlán (Morelos) and Huejotzingo (Puebla), both about an hour from Mexico City. Also in Acapulco.

February 2—Dia de la Candelaria ("Candelaria" means Candlemas)—for die-hards the end of the Christmas season. Final appearances of Christ as a child until the following Dec.

February 5—Constitution Day, a national holiday.

February 19—Cuautla, Morelos, celebrates the breaking of Spanish siege of city during the War of Independence in early 1800's. All-out fiesta.

March-April (variable date)—Holy Week, widely observed with special passion play presentations all over Mexico, especially in Taxco, state of Guerrero (all week); in Ixtapalapa, Mexico City, on Good Friday.

March 21—A national holiday celebrating birth of Benito Juarez, heroic 19th-century president.

May 1—Labor Day, a national holiday; workers parade in the capital and most other cities.

May 3—La Santa Cruz (The Holy Cross)—Fair and folk dances in Milpa Alta, of the Federal District.

May 5—*Cinco de Mayo,* anniversary of French defeat at Puebla; start of month-long fair in Puebla.

May 10—Mother's Day, not an official holiday, but many businesses close for a half-day and restaurants are crowded.

May-June (variable date)—Corpus Christi Day. In Mexico City children, including babes in arms, are dressed in native costumes and taken to the cathedral on the *zocalo* for blessing. Afterward they'll pose for anyone in and about the *zocalo*—it's a field day for the photographer, amateur and professional.

ne—*Tianguis Turistico,* a big trade show for the travel industry, held for four days in Acapulco; dates vary.

une 1—Navy Day, celebrated in all of the more important parts in the country and very big in Acapulco.

une 24—Dia de San Juan (St. John the Baptist)—anywhere in Mexico you might get doused with a bucket of water.

uly 28—Tlalpan, Federal District—Traditional Fair dates back to colonial days held in main square. Southern outskirts of Mexico City.

ugust 15–16—Huamantla, Tlaxcala—Annual fair with exhibits of regional handicrafts, wool-woven products, features beautiful carpets made of flowers and sawdust "paving" the streets. On Highway 136.

ugust 21—Dances all day at Cuauhtémoc Circle on Reforma Blvd., Mexico City—also on Aug. 13.

ugust 23—San Bartolo Naucalpan, State of Mexico—(An industrial suburb of Mexico City on NW outskirts), another traditional fete with all the trimmings.

ugust 28—Puebla—Festival of St. Augustine, dazzling fireworks, city decorated with colorful paper hangings, seasonal fruits and nuts abundant.

eptember 6–9—Cholula, Pue.—Festival of Our Lady of the Remedies featuring native dances in the atrium of that church, sitting atop largest pyramid in the world. Highway 190, 9 miles this side of Puebla.

eptember 7–8—Nativity of the Virgin Mary in Tepoztlán, state of Morelos.

eptember 16—Independence Day—starts the night before when all over Mexico public officials give the "grito," Father Hidalgo's original cry for independence.

eptember (last Sunday)—Fiesta of Atlixcáyotl in Atlixco, Puebla, with exhibitions of traditional regional dances. Very colorful. From Mexico City, #150/150D to Puebla, marked turnoff to Atlixco.

)ctober 12—Columbus Day (Día de la Raza).

November 1–2—All Souls' Day and Day of the Dead—in Mixquic, Federal District, and much of provincial Mexico, candlelit all-night vigils at cemeteries, graves decorated.

November 20—Anniversary of the Mexican Revolution.

November (last week, or early Dec.)—Silver fair in Taxco, Guerrero.

)ecember—*Nao de China* (China Ship) fair during first two weeks in Acapulco, marks anniversary of when the ships came in from the Orient during colonial times.

)ecember 12—Día de Guadalupe (Day of Our Lady of Guadalupe), Mexico's patroness saint, observed all over the country, but especially at the shrine in Mexico City with processions, native folk dances, etc.

)ecember 16–25—Christmas season, widely observed all over the country with *posada* processions leading to Christmas parties, nativity plays, fireworks. Mexico City is decorated throughout like a brilliant Christmas tree.

BUSINESS HOURS AND HOLIDAY CLOSINGS. Banks are open from 9 A.M. to 1:30 P.M. Monday through Friday. In Mexico City some banks open Saturday mornings. Stores in the capital usually are open 10 A.M.–6 P.M., in Acapulco, 10 A.M.–8 P.M., but close from 1 or 2 until 4 or 5 P.M.

TRAVELING WITH PETS. Not recommended. If you choose to travel with a pet, you must have a statement of good health from a licensed veterinarian that is certified by a Mexican consul.

HOTELS. Hotels and other accommodations in this guide are divided into categories, arranged primarily by price. These categories are *Gran Turismo,* (where the visitor can expect all amenities in a special, luxurious atmosphere, particularly in the larger cities and posh resort areas); *Deluxe; Expensive; Moderate,* and *Inexpensive.* Costs are given for a double room and exclude tips and other extras.

Note: Hotel rates are set and approved by the *Government Tourist Secretariat;* no hotel can raise its prices without official permission. However, due to inflation, hotel rates are raised frequently to meet increased costs. Current approved rates are posted in each hotel room.

 DINING OUT. Mexico City and Acapulco have most of the best restaurants in the country. Both places have full range of cafes featuring ethnic cuisines: Italian, French, Cantonese, Japanese, and, of course, Mexican. Acapulco, understandably, is especially good when it comes to seafood. The cost of dining out varies widely, but in Mexico it will be less than a similar establishment in the United States. The one exception occurs when ordering anything imported, such as wine, whiskey, or salmon. These go for double U.S. prices.

Expensive restaurants are easy to find. Both Mexico City and Acapulco have a number of U.S.-style fast food outlets which are easy on the budget.

Even cheaper are small beaneries in Mexico City where you can get a set menu with some choices (it's called *comida corrida*) for very little. If a place looks clean and its customers fairly well dressed, it probably won't cause any tummy troubles. Still, in Acapulco, where heat is a problem, small cafes off the Costera Boulevard should be avoided.

In Mexico City the drill is a big breakfast and a hefty lunch in mid-afternoon followed by a small supper. Tourists may prefer a light lunch and big dinner. Be prepared to eat late; show up at a restaurant before 8 P.M. and you may be the only customer. Acapulco goes in for light lunches and big dinners (many of the more elegant spots open evenings only). Reservations usually are a good idea.

Credit cards are in wide use in the better restaurants. Ask if yours is accepted when you make a reservation. Most places that accept the Mexican *Bancomer* credit card will also accept *Visa; Carnet* in Mexico corresponds to *Mastercard* and *Banamex* to *Masterchage.*

 TIPPING. Baffling in any foreign currency, tipping is even more confusing in Mexico with its high inflation and constantly devaluing peso. Restaurants are easy 10%–15% of the bill. Elsewhere, keep the exchange rate in mind (what, at the moment, is the equivalent of a dollar, and hand out pesos accordingly.

The following is a suggested guide for individuals:

Waiters—15% of restaurant or bar bill.

Bellboys—At least half-a-dollar for one or two bags, a quarter for each additional bag.

Porters—Same as above.

Hotel maids—Minimum of a half-a-dollar a day.

Taxis—a tip is not expected, although many passengers give the driver the small change left over from the fare.

Ushers at major shows or sporting events—a quarter.

Parking policemen and car-watchers a dime to a quarter per hour parked, and usually same per hour (important to remember when visiting museums and the like).

Shoeshine boys—their fee, not a tip.

Tourist guides—for meeting service for 1 or 2 persons at airport or railroad station, $1 U.S. per person. For ½-day tour (3 to 4 hrs.), $2 U.S. per person; full day, $4 U.S. per person. Use your own judgment for longer trips (a week or two, for instance); much will depend on your guide's service and general excellence. A fair tip for a 6-day tour would be $20–$24 U.S. per person.

Bus groups, in addition to tipping their guide, usually make up a small pool for the driver. Not essential, but always much appreciated.

Additional tipping hints: Always try to carry with you a bunch of 20- and 50-peso coins. Don't overtip. Learn immediately on arrival *to think in pesos* and not in dollars. The minimum wage in Mexico is about 50 U.S. cents per hour.

SHOPPING. The sentence has been repeated so often it's become a cliché, but it's absolutely true, nonetheless: Mexico is a shopper's paradise. It's the land where the beautiful or unusual item lovingly created and decorated by hand is still considered king—where new materials, paints, and finishes are, often reluctantly, adopted only where they enhance the final effect of traditional, time-honored designs. It's the land, too, of the small, family-run handicraft workshop where quality, not quantity, remains the watchword.

It's also inhabited, unfortunately, by the entrepreneur who turns out cheap, shoddy merchandise masquerading as "native handicraft" to satisfy the souvenir hunter looking for a bargain. The shopper needs a discerning eye to sort out the chaff, selecting only those pieces worth buying and carrying home to treasure.

Bargaining? Of course. It's a game of fluctuating values that can be played to the hilt with roadside vendors and in the native markets. Some items sold by Indians at street-side in and around Mexico City are so low in price that it's a shame to even try bargaining—they are so poor and, in comparison, you are so rich. In Acapulco, it's just the opposite—they overcharge. Try offering half of the asking price and come up very slowly. Unless you just must have the item, never pay more than 70% of the asking price. Show interest but not too much. Walking away will almost always result in your last offer being accepted. Shops have fixed prices but it can't hurt to ask for a discount; you can often get 10% off at all but the most exclusive shops. For U.S. Customs purposes, Mexico is classified as a "developing" country. This means that many of its local products may enter the U.S. entirely free of Customs duties, that they do not count on your $300 exemption. Since the list of products is long, and is reviewed every year, you should write to: Department of the Treasury, U.S. Customs Service, Washington, D.C. 20229, for the latest edition of the brochure, *GSP & the Traveler.*

Driving down through Mexico, one finds woolen serapes, rugs, in Saltillo. Certain villages in this state weave rebozos only of silk (a rebozo is the Mexican version of the stole), some of them reputedly of such fine thread they can be slipped through a woman's finger ring.

Semiprecious stones—delicately purple amethysts, opals in a range of colors —are found in the Querétaro region. You will be approached here by ambulatory vendors who bring handkerchief-wrapped stones out of their pockets, but confine your purchases to reputable stores in town to be sure of the quality.

Toluca, one of the highest cities in the country (8,710 feet), offers at its Friday market a bewildering array of handloomed cloth, serapes, baskets of all shapes and sizes, jewelry of bone, fiber rugs and mats, and reed furniture, among many others.

Nearby Metepec is noted for its "trees-of-life" and other ceramic figures, as well as cooking pottery of all types. Puebla produces fine ceramic ware in shades of blue, yellow, and white and is famous for its Talavera tiles.

Taxco produces fine silver jewelry and table items, as well as "wedded metal" ware (silver and brass) in a variety of styles—traditional or modern Mexican, Danish modern, some even Oriental in feel. Don't buy cheap silver—yes, it's available. Good silver is not pliable in the fingers, and the products of all reputable factories (many of them small home affairs) bear the stamp of a spread eagle—the hallmark of Mexican sterling. Taxco also produces a line of fine ceramics.

Cuernavaca and Acapulco shops feature smart resort wear for men and women—tailored pants, pantsuits, simple dresses—both short and long—with stunning embroidery, lacy beach coats and sun hats, and the popular *chaleco* jacket—a cotton, pleated-front, long-sleeved sport shirt (girls use them for beach jackets).

Government-run handicraft shops as well as Woolworth's (yes, *the* Woolworth's) and Sanborn's in Mexico City and Acapulco, have a good selection of items—pottery, textiles, copper, wrought iron, and more), all at attractive prices.

 TIME ZONES. Mexico City and Acapulco are on Central Standard Time throughout the year. In the summer keep in mind Central Standard is the same as Mountain Daylight.

Mountain Standard—Baja California south from Santa Rosalia; west coast of mainland south to, but not including, Puerto Vallarta.

If you are vacationing in Mexico during Daylight Savings summer months in the United States and wish to make a phone call to the Eastern U.S., remember that their clocks are 2 hours ahead from the bulk of Mexico.

 ELECTRIC CURRENT. All Mexico is on 60-cycle, 120 voltage current. This means that your small electric appliances (shaver, hair dryer, electric hair-rollers, etc.) will operate as well and as safely anywhere in Mexico as they do at home. Plugs are the same as in the U.S. but you might want to take an extension cord, as outlets are not always conveniently located.

In any event, we advise that both men and women carry with them a hand razor for emergency use when the electric power goes off—which happens frequently even in Mexico City, not to mention Acapulco. Nobody understands exactly why, but that's the reason every hotel and motel room is equipped with a candle. Just in case you wondered! Power failures are most frequent during the violent downpours of the rainy season—and this happens in all parts of Mexico.

 TELEPHONES. The country's telephone system works most of the time, but as there are too few lines, you might have to wait a bit to get through during peak business hours in Mexico City. Local calls can be dialed from most hotels, but long distance requires operator assistance. Naturally, there is a service charge. It is often cheaper to make your international call from a long-distance concessionary, called *caseta de large distancia*. The problem is hat they are sometimes hard to find and it's unlikely that much English will be spoken.

To call Mexico City from the United States dial area code 905 and the number; to reach Acapulco dial 01152714 and then the local number. Within the country the area code for Mexico City is 915, for Acapulco 91714. To call the U.S. from Mexico, dial 95 and the area code, or dial 09 for an English-speaking international operator who will assist you (collect calls, as they are not subject to hefty Mexican taxes, are less expensive than calling direct, but the caller is subject to a service charge if the call is not accepted or the person called cannot be reached). Domestic long-distance operators in Mexico (who rarely speak English) may be reached by dialing 02.

The government owns and runs the telephone system with no competition. Collect calls are usually accepted only to the U.S., Britain and a few European countries. Within Mexico, long-distance calls are more reasonable, but still expensive by U.S. standards. In a person-to-person call (national or international), you will be charged the equivalent of a one-minute station call, even if the party you asked for is not there. This is to prevent cheating by the use of some previously agreed-upon code.

Local calls from a coin booth cost only one peso.

LAUNDRY AND DRY CLEANING. First class and better hotels provide same-day service. Mexico City has laundries and cleaners as well as laundromats; if you are staying in a small hotel, ask for a recommendation. Small hotels in Acapulco can arrange for laundry and dry cleaning, but two or three days may pass between pickup and delivery.

SENIOR CITIZEN/STUDENT TRAVEL. Senior citizens should always have an identification card with them, even though resort areas do not generally offer any special discounts. All student travelers should obtain an *International Student Identity Card,* which is in most instances needed to get student discounts, youth rail passes, and Intra-European student charter flights. Apply to *Council On International Educational Exchange,* 205 East 42 St., New York, NY 10017, 212–661–1414, or 312 Sutter St., San Francisco, CA 94108, 415–421–3472. Canadian students should apply to the *Association of Student Councils,* 44 St. George St., Toronto, Ontario M5S QE4, 416–979–2604.

The following organizations can also be helpful in finding student flights, educational opportunities, and other information. Most deal with international student travel generally, but materials offered by those listed do cover Mexico.

Council on International Educational Exchange (CIEE), 205 East 42 St., New York, NY 10017, 212–661–1414; and 312 Sutter St., San Francisco, CA 94108, 415–421–3472, provides information on summer study, work/travel programs, and travel services for college and high school students, and a free charter flights guide booklet. Their *Whole World Handbook* ($6.95 plus $1 postage) is the best listing of both work and study possibilities.

Institute of International Education, 809 United Nations Plaza, New York, NY 10017, 212–883–8200 is primarily concerned with study opportunities and administers scholarships and fellowships for international study and training. The New York office has a counseling service and library; satellite offices are located in Chicago, Denver, Houston, San Francisco, and Washington. *Vacation*

Study Abroad is an annually revised guide to over 900 courses offered by both foreign and American colleges and universities. *U.S. College-Sponsored Programs Abroad* gives details on foreign study programs run by American schools, for academic credit. These publications are $9.95 each, including first-class postage and handling.

Arista Student Travel Assoc., Inc., 1 Rockefeller Plaza, New York, NY 10020, 212–541–9190, is a specialist in the field of youth travel, offering student and young adult tours.

Your World Travel Services, Inc., 2050 West Good Hope Road, Milwaukee, WI 53209–2889, 414–351–6363, has an eight-day tour to Mexico for students.

Specific information and rail and other discounts are listed in the appropriate sections.

In Canada: *AOSC (Association of Student Councils),* 44 St. George St., Toronto, Ontario M5S 2E4, 416–979–2604 is a nonprofit student service cooperative owned and operated by over 50 college and university student unions. Its travel bureau provides transportation tours and work camps worldwide.

HANDICAPPED TRAVEL. *Access to the World: A Travel Guide for the Handicapped,* by Louise Weiss, is an outstanding book that covers all aspects of travel for anyone with health or medical problems; it features extensive listings and suggestions on everything from availability of special diets to wheelchair accessibility. Order from Facts on File, 460 Park Ave. South, New York, NY 10003 ($14.95).

Tours specially designed for the handicapped generally parallel those of the nonhandicapped traveler, but at a more leisurely pace. For a complete list of tour operators who arrange such travel, write to the *Society for the Advancement of Travel for the Handicapped,* 26 Court St., Brooklyn, NY 11242. Another excellent source of information is *Rehabilitation International U.S.A.,* 1123 Broadway, New York, NY 10010, which publishes the "International Directory of Access Guides." *Moss Rehabilitation Hospital,* 12th St. and Tabor Rd., Philadelphia, PA 19141, answers inquiries regarding specific cities and countries and provides toll-free telephone numbers for airlines that have special lines for the hearing impaired. They also have listings of selected tour operators.

International Air Transport Association (IATA) publishes a free pamphlet entitled "Incapacitated Passengers' Air Travel Guide" that explains the various arrangements to be made and how to make them. Write IATA, 2000 Teel Street, Montreal, Quebec H3A 2R4.

HEALTH. All hotels, even the cheapest, have physicians they can call in. Acapulco has fair hospitals, but those in Mexico City are on a par with some of the best in the world. Air ambulances are available for those preferring to be cared for in the United States.

Digestive upsets and diarrhea are the most frequent complaints. Often these can be avoided by eating and drinking sparingly; Mexico City's 7,200-foot altitude and Acapulco's tropical climate require the body to do more adjusting than most people realize.

Victims of what has been called Montezuma's Revenge—watery stools, abdominal cramps, nausea, and possibly fever—should consult the hotel physician. That way the trouble usually can be cleared up in a day. Different symptoms call for different medications, which make self-treatment a bit of a gamble.

Health and Medical Supplies

1. Carry with you on your trip a small supply of whatever medical products you customarily use at home—aspirin, throat lozenges, vitamins, and such. The same brands may not be available in Mexico.

2. If some of the above are on prescription, be sure to have the prescription with you and handy to show at the border on your return trip to the U.S., or the American customs agents may seize your pills or powders.

3. Tetanus and typhoid shots are not required, but, if they make you feel safer, have them administered well before your departure from home. Also gamma globulin to prevent hepatitis (maybe) if you plan on going to out-of-the-way places.

4. If you wear prescription glasses, prescription sunglasses, or contact lenses, be sure to carry one extra pair of each with you, as well as a copy of your eye prescription.

5. If you have a serious medical problem of any kind (like diabetes or epilepsy), wear a neck or wrist tag to this effect—a *MedicAlert* tag is good.

6. Be sure to carry with you an identification card showing whom to notify in case of serious illness or death, your Social Security number, and identification card for any insurance, especially medical. It's also a good idea to note your blood type on the ID card, especially if yours is a rare type.

7. Many English-speaking doctors, dentists and other specialists live in Mexico. U.S. Embassy in Mexico City has a list of approved physicians. Call 553–3333 day or night. Same at the British Embassy, 511–4880.

Mosquito and other nuisance bites can be prevented by liberal applications of insect repellant. If you get bitten, an antihistamine cream can reduce swelling and itching. Rubbing wet soap on a bite and letting it dry is also good first-aid for itching. There have been recent cases of malaria on the southern Pacific coast and in a few other areas, so ask your doctor about prophylactic quinine tablets. In Mexico, you can purchase malaria-preventive Aralen without a prescription. These tablets should be taken regularly, according to instructions, before entering a malarial region.

POSTAGE. Rates are reasonable, but often increase without advance notice to compensate for inflation. As a result, this frequently requires sticking several stamps on a postcard or envelope. Post office hours are from 8 A.M. to 6 P.M. It takes about a week for an airmail letter to reach the U.S., and some two weeks to Europe.

ENGLISH LANGUAGE MEDIA. *The News,* published in Mexico City, is a good general newspaper distributed in larger cities and resorts. There's an occasional undubbed English-language film on TV but just about everything else on TV is in Spanish. Mexico City has an English-language FM radio station, affiliated with CBS. Many hotels in Mexico City and Acapulco pick up U.S. television programs beamed by satellite.

AIRPORT DEPARTURE TAXES. On international flights US $10, or the current equivalent in pesos, to be paid prior to boarding; on domestic flights the airport tax is included in the ticket price.

International flights open for check-in two hours before departure time. It is suggested that you arrive early, as reserved seats are given on a first-come, first-served basis. Many flights have open seating and Mexican politeness does not extend to queues. During holidays, airports are madhouses and waiting lists are long. On crowded flights, even confirmed reservations can be cancelled if you don't show up at least 60 min. before departure. Although not quite as punctual as their U.S. or European counterparts, Mexican flights usually do leave on time. Don't plan on tight connections, because your checked luggage might not accompany you. On domestic flights there is a penalty, sometimes up to 50% of the ticket price, charged to no-shows. When you are booked on a flight, try not to miss it.

 CUSTOMS. U.S. residents may bring in $400 worth of foreign merchandise as gifts or for personal use without having to pay duty, provided they have been out of the country more than 48 hours and provided they have not claimed a similar exemption within the previous 30 days. Every member of a family is entitled to the same exemption, regardless of age, and the exemptions can be pooled. For the next $1,000 worth of goods a flat 10% rate is assessed.

Included in the $400 allowance for travelers over the age of 21 are one liter of alcohol, 100 non-Cuban cigars and 200 cigarettes. Only one bottle of perfume trademarked in the U.S. may be brought in. However, there is no duty on antiques or art over 100 years old. You may not bring home meats, fruits, plants, soil or other agricultural products.

Gifts valued at under $50 may be mailed to friends or relatives at home, but not more than one per day of receipt to any one addressee. These gifts must not include perfumes costing more than $5, tobacco or liquor.

Canada. In addition to personal effects, and over and above the regular exemption of $150 per year, the following may be brought into Canada duty-free: a maximum of 50 cigars, 200 cigarettes, 2 pounds of tobacco and 40 ounces of liquor, provided these are declared in writing to customs on arrival. Canadian customs regulations are strictly enforced; you are advised to check what your allowances are and to make sure you have kept receipts for whatever you may have brought abroad. Small gifts can be mailed and should be marked "unsolicited gift, value under $25 in Canadian funds." (You should also include the nature of the gift.) For other details ask for the Canada Customs brochure "I Declare."

British residents. Returning from Mexico (or any other non-E.E.C. country), you may import duty free: 200 cigarettes or 100 cigarillos or 50 cigars or 250 grammes of tobacco (*Note* if you live outside Europe, these allowances are doubled); plus one liter of alcoholic drinks over 22% vol. (38.8% proof) or two liters of alcoholic drinks not over 22% vol. or fortified or sparkling wine; plus two liters of still table wine; plus 50 grammes of perfume; plus nine fluid ounces of toilet water; plus other goods to the value of £28.

In addition, no animals or pets of any kind may be brought into the U.K. The penalties for doing so are severe and are strictly enforced; there are *no* exceptions. Similarly, fresh meats, plants and vegetables, controlled drugs and firearms and ammunition may not be brought into the U.K. There are no restrictions on the import or export of British and foreign currencies.

MEXICO CITY AND ENVIRONS

The City That IS Mexico

by
JIM BUDD

Jim Budd, Mexico City bureau chief for Murdoch Magazines (Travel
Weekly, Meetings & Conventions, *and* Incentive World), *has lived in
the Mexican capital since 1958. A former editor of the* Mexico City
News *and the Spanish-language business magazine* Expansión, *he has
concentrated on travel writing for the past fifteen years.*

Founded by the Aztecs in 1325, Mexico City is the oldest capital in
the New World. Of late is also has become the center of the largest
metropolitan area on earth. According to some estimates as many as
18 million people live crowded into the Valley of Mexico at a breathtaking altitude of more than 7,000 feet.

To the people of the country, Mexico City is Mexico. That is what
they call it, simply "México." The rest of the nation is "La Republica,"
The Republic.

Yet, technically speaking, Mexico City does not exist. It is the Feder-

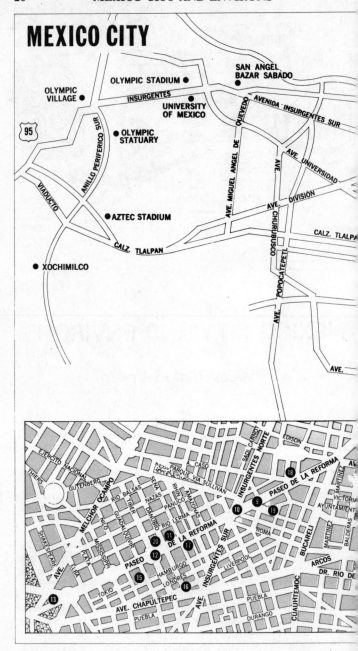

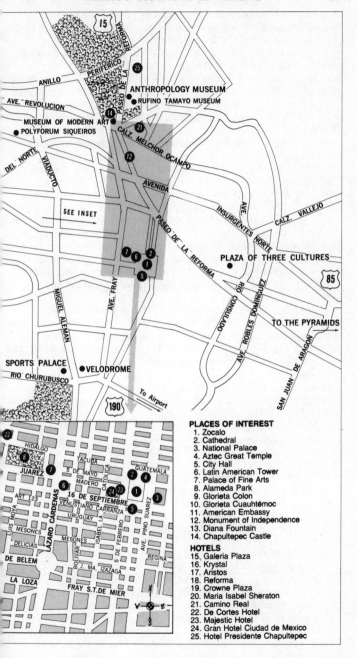

PLACES OF INTEREST
1. Zocalo
2. Cathedral
3. National Palace
4. Aztec Great Temple
5. City Hall
6. Latin American Tower
7. Palace of Fine Arts
8. Alameda Park
9. Glorieta Colon
10. Glorieta Cuauhtémoc
11. American Embassy
12. Monument of Independence
13. Diana Fountain
14. Chapultepec Castle

HOTELS
15. Galeria Plaza
16. Krystal
17. Aristos
18. Reforma
19. Crowne Plaza
20. Maria Isabel Sheraton
21. Camino Real
22. De Cortes Hotel
23. Majestic Hotel
24. Gran Hotel Ciudad de Mexico
25. Hotel Presidente Chapultepec

al District or *Distrito Federal,* governed directly by the President of the Republic through a mayor he appoints. Next door, to add to the confusion, is the State of Mexico with all its many suburbs.

To the south lies Cuernavaca, that "sunny spot for shady people" which at 5,000 feet is a tropical weekend haven for the capital's wealthy. Beyond is Taxco, a silvermining town of cobbled lanes and whitewashed houses roofed with tile. Taxco is picturebook Mexico. East is Puebla, regal and Iberian. North are the Pyramids at San Juan de Teotihuacan. North, too, are the ruins at Tula, fabled capital of the Toltecs.

Most of what is now Mexico has been ruled from the central valleys for time immemorial.

Teotihuacan was a contemporary of Imperial Rome, but an even grander city. Too big and too grand perhaps. Some 1,500 years ago it was the heart of an empire that extended nearly from Texas to Guatemala. No one can really say what led to its fall.

Best guess is that Teotihuacan was overrun by barbaric hordes from the north. These may have been the Toltecs, warriors who forged a great empire of their own a millenium ago. The Toltecs, too, are a vanished people. Many migrated to Yucatan where they conquered the Maya city states only to be absorbed by the people they had vanquished. Once again, it appears, barbaric hordes from the north drove them out.

The Aztecs, who called themselves Mexicas and claimed to have come from a place called Aztlán, were part of this horde. Miserable nomads who settled on what was then an island in a lake, the Aztecs arrived in the 14th century and within a hundred years or so had defeated their neighbors and established a realm that spanned the continent.

It was to overthrow the Aztec regime that thousands of Indians allied themselves in 1520 with Hernan Cortés and his little band of adventurers. On the rubble of Montezuma's halls arose a new Mexico City, capital of New Spain, famed as the city of palaces and in the 1700s the grandest metropolis in the New World.

Three centuries of foreign rule came to an end with the uprisings in 1810. What had been New Spain became a free nation, taking the name of its Aztec-founded capital city. Yet independence brought with it decades of turmoil. A brief attempt to place the government in the hands of a European prince failed and cost Austria's Maximilian his life. Thirty years of dictatorship followed, ending with the Revolution of 1910 that ousted Porfirio Díaz. Modern Mexico was born in that revolution.

Mexico City today is a capsule of eons of history. Glorified is the ancient past, magnificent murals lauding the achievements of long ago, statues of Aztec rulers standing on the boulevards. Nor is Spain forgotten. The downtown area, formally decreed the Historic Center, is one great outdoor museum of palaces and churches from the Iberian era.

But most of all Mexico City is modern. A vibrant capital that rarely slumbers, it is a metropolis of fine shops, wonderful restaurants, magnificent museums and tree-shaded avenues. One of the most exciting metropolises in the world, it is a promise of an afternoon at the races, an evening at the jai alai games, a night at the discos. It is watching the spectacular Ballet Folklorico at nine in the morning, enjoying a mariachi serenade while being poled through the floating gardens at Xochimilco, and then thrilling to the daring of a matador at the bullfights.

Shopping often is the high point of a vacation; it always is in Mexico City, where one can start the day haggling at a native market and end it negotiating a discount at an elegant Pink Zone boutique. Not that haggling or negotiating are necessary; these days any price quoted in Mexico City is a bargain.

The art is breathtaking. The vivid colors of the murals at University City are never to be forgotten. Striking are the canvases displayed at outdoor exhibits on Saturdays and Sundays, as well as those at the posh galleries on Reforma and Juarez.

Then, for a change of pace, there are the day trips that may be extended to overnight excursions to Taxco, Puebla, or the many other nearby points. Especially nice are brief holidays at the hacienda resorts. Back in the days before agrarian reform, haciendas were vast plantations, estates the size of dukedoms, where owners lived in regal splendor. Many of those stately homes have been converted into splendid hotels in the country, complete with tennis courts, bridle trails, and golf links, most of them little more than an hour's drive from the city.

Eventually, of course, the bright lights lure back the restless. The capital really is a destination in itself. Smog there is, to be sure, and traffic jams. Residents grumble about overcrowding and much more, but visitors scarcely notice. They are too busy having a good time. Ancient and grand, modern and dynamic, Mexico City is one of the most fascinating cities on earth.

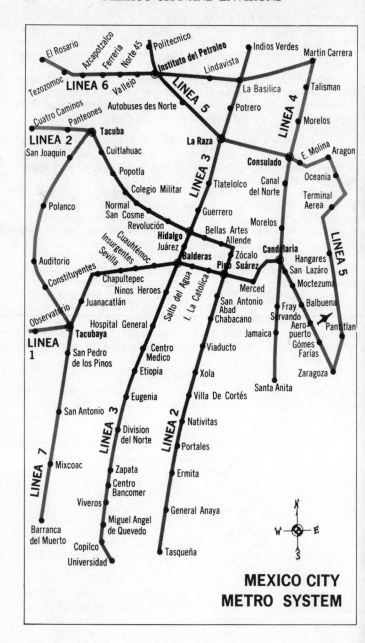

MEXICO CITY METRO SYSTEM

EXPLORING MEXICO CITY

Large as it is, Mexico City need not be an especially confusing town. The main street, Reforma Boulevard, runs roughly eastward from Chapultepec Park for some 30 blocks, becomes Avenida Juarez for ten blocks, and finally Avenida Madero which, after five blocks spills into the huge plaza called the Zocalo. Most hotels are located along this axis or near it.

The Zocalo, largest square in the Americas, is the traditional heart of Mexico City. Just north of it are the recently uncovered remains of the Great Temple of the Aztecs. On the plaza itself is the National Palace; supposedly it was begun on orders of Hernan Cortés and later became the hall from which the viceroys reigned. Towering above it is the magnificent Metropolitan Cathedral, built to show God's glory is greater than man's. For blocks around all is colonial splendor, a monument to 300 years of Spanish rule.

Avenida Madero, narrow, crowded, yet picturesque and charming, is perhaps the most lovely of the ancient streets. At its western end it comes crashing into the 20th century at the big blue Latin American Tower. The tower, at 44 stories no longer the tallest building in the city, is still a good place from which to get a feel for the Valley of Mexico. Admission to the observation floors on the top costs about a dollar.

Beyond the tower and across busy Lazaro Cardenas, Madero becomes Juarez. Notable landmark is the Palace of Fine Arts, and farther on the Alameda Park. Some 25 or 30 years ago Juarez was the most fashionable shopping street in town, but over the years the more posh boutiques and cafes have moved westward.

Reforma Boulevard, once residential, has become the smart address for today's better shops, restaurants, hotels, and office towers. Those not on Reforma strive to be near it in the few blocks bounded by Niza, Florencia, and Avenida Chapultepec, the trendy neighborhood known for some obscure reason as the Pink Zone or the *Zona Rosa.*

Reforma itself was laid out along the lines of Paris' Champs d'Élysées by order of Emperor Maximilian. During his brief reign in the 1860s the ill-fated Austrian converted the castle in Chapultepec Park into his imperial residence. From there he was wont to ride grandly in state to his offices in the National Palace on the Zocalo.

Midway along its length, Reforma is intersected by Avenida Insurgentes. Running roughly north and south, Insurgentes is the only street that actually bisects the city. To the north is the Basilica of Guadalupe, holiest shrine in the country. Beyond are the grand pyramids and all that remains of the great vanished civilization called Teotihuacan. Insurgentes Sur (*sur* meaning south) becomes the capital's restaurant row. It leads to San Angel, a charmingly colonial residential area. The bull ring is out this way, as is University City. Those who continue onward eventually will reach Cuernavaca and Taxco.

EXPLORING THE ENVIRONS OF MEXICO CITY

The Cuernavaca–Taxco route long has been a favorite with those venturing outside Mexico City.

Less than 50 miles from Mexico City, Cuernavaca, legend has it, has been a resort since Aztec times. Lower in altitude, at 5,000 feet, it is tropical without being oppressively hot. The locals claim Cuernavaca has the best climate in the world. Cortes built himself a palace there and conquerors of all sorts have been following his example ever since. Tycoons weekend in Cuernavaca, princes holiday there, and Americans have made it a retirement community. Tourists delight in sampling its many pleasant inns and restaurants.

Taxco, about a 90-minute drive farther on, is more the postcard Mexico one hopes to find south of the border. Cuernavaca at first glance is an ugly place; it hides its beauty behind walls. Taxco, on the other hand, is a winner from the moment it is first glimpsed, all red-tiled and whitewashed, clinging to the hills. Silver is what brings people to Taxco. The ore has been mined there since colonial times, but it was only half a century ago that New Orleans' Bill Spratling brought his jewelry-making techniques to the village. Scores of little silver shops remain as a monument to Spratling's having lived and taught there.

Two roads lead north out of Mexico City, one being the old Pan American Highway (Route 85) and the other the Queretaro Turnpike (Highway 57). A nice circle trip is heading up 85 and turning off to see the Pyramids at Teotihuacan along the way and possibly overnighting there. Then a night can be spent in Pachuca, a pretty little mining town not many travelers take the time to see. Nice up this way is San Miguel Regla, a resort in the mountains. From Pachuca a back road cuts over to Tula where the ruins of the ancient capital of the Toltecs are to be seen. Tula is just off the turnpike that heads back toward Mexico City.

East, about 80 miles away, is Puebla. While it can easily enough be visited in a day, spending a couple of nights is not a bad idea. There is much to see, from the splendid baroque churches that are in themselves works of art to the huge, still-buried pyramid at Cholula and lions and tigers roaming free at Africam, a zoo that is not a zoo. Beyond Puebla is Tehuacan, the spa town from which most of Mexico's bottled water comes and where some still seek cures.

PRACTICAL INFORMATION FOR MEXICO CITY AND ENVIRONS

 HOW TO GET THERE. All roads, railways and air routes (well, nearly all) within Mexico lead to Mexico City. Most international visitors these days arrive by plane; few U.S. gateway cities are even as much as five hours flying time from the capital. By road from the closest U.S. border points the trip takes a day and a half (20 hours driving time or more). Trains are even slower.

By Air. From the U.S., *Aeroméxico* flies into Mexico City from Atlanta, Houston, Los Angeles, Miami, New York, and Tucson while *Mexicana* flies from Chicago, Dallas/Fort Worth, Denver, Los Angeles, Miami, Philadelphia, San Antonio, San Francisco, San Juan, and Seattle. U.S. carriers serving Mexico City include *American Airlines, Braniff, Continental, Pan American* and *Western.* From the rest of the world airlines flying into Mexico City are *Air France, Air Panama, Aeroflot, Aerolineas Argentinas, Aeronica, Aeroperu, Avianca, Aviateca, Iberia, Japan Air Lines, KLM, Lacsa, Lufthansa, Taca, Tan,* and *Viasa.*

From Canada, *Japan Air Lines* flies in thrice weekly out of Vancouver while *Iberia* comes in from Montreal and *Aeroméxico* operates one flight a week out of Toronto.

Promotional fares in an almost endless variety frequently are available. Tour packages usually include substantial air fare discounts. Often considerable savings may be made by flying from border points within Mexico. Airline tour packages purchased within Mexico also can be quite attractive. Bear in mind, however, that no-shows lose 50% of the ticket price in penalties on Mexican domestic flights.

By Bus. Travel by bus in Mexico is quite cheap; however, you get what you pay for and little more. Even for those fluent in Spanish it can be confusing, and the garbled platform announcements are made only in Spanish. Passengers desiring to stop over en route should buy a ticket only to the city where they wish to stop and on arrival reserve a seat aboard the bus they wish to depart on; this costs no more. The good side of bus travel, aside from saving money, is the opportunity to see and get the feel of the country.

From **Matamoros** (across from Brownsville) the trip to Mexico City takes about 14 hours; from **Laredo** 15 hours; from **Ciudad Juarez** (El Paso) 24 hours; from **Nogales** 40 hours; from **Tijuana** 44 hours. Buses depart these border cities every hour on the hour from 6 A.M. until 10 P.M.

By Train. Slower and cheaper (sleeping births are extra) are the railroads which are operated by the government as a social service. Again you get what you pay for. Bring food and be prepared to tip the conductor to help you find the space you have booked. From **Laredo** the trip takes 24 hours; from **Juarez** 36 hours; from **Nogales** and **Mexicali** allow two days. Trains often arrive many hours behind schedule.

By Car. Driving time from the border is about the same as it is for the buses, which really roll along. Highways are fair to good, although in most cases only two lanes. Distances between towns are considerable. It is wise to top off the tank at every opportunity. It also is wise to drive only during daylight hours when the roads are patrolled by the *Green Angels,* who are out to watch for motorists in distress (cattle, among other things, make nighttime driving dangerous). Buy Mexican insurance at the border; uninsured drivers involved in accidents can wind up in jail. While speed limits usually do not exist, pretend they do and hold the line at 55; you won't regret it. Directional signs at times are lacking; when in doubt, ask. A questioning "MeHEEco?" (as everyone calls Mexico City) should bring either a nod or a finger pointing in another direction. No matter where on the border you are coming from you almost certainly will arrive via Queretaro on Highway 57. This is an expressway that passes through miles of suburbs. Turn off at the *Reforma Centro* ("centro" means downtown) exit and you will be headed for the heart of the city.

 EMERGENCY TELEPHONE NUMBERS. The area code for Mexico City is 5; for Cuernavaca 731; for Pachuca 771; for Puebla 22; for Taxco 732 and for Tehuacan 238. Within Mexico dial 91 for access to long distance lines. To call Mexico from abroad first dial 01152.

Only local calls can be dialed directly from hotels. International calls should be made collect whenever possible in order to avoid exhorbitant Mexican taxes and hefty hotel service charges.

Calls from public telephones cost only a peso, an exceptional bargain. From public phones long distance calls must be made collect. Dial 09 to reach an international operator (they speak English as well as Spanish) and 02 for domestic calls (operators speak only Spanish). Directory assistance is 04; only Spanish is spoken.

Emergencies are best handled through hotels; people on the staff know both the ropes and the language. *Locatel,* 658–1111, is the general emergency number in Mexico City, but its operators speak only Spanish. When there is nowhere else to turn, dial 09, international long distance; these operators do speak English and should be able to summon help.

The *American-British Cowdray Hospital,* also known as the *ABC* and the *Hospital Inglés,* has English-speaking personnel on its staff and can handle any emergency medical situation for a price. Telephone 277–5000. The *Mexican Red Cross,* 557–5758, has its own hospital and ambulance fleet; there are no charges for its services but personnel seldom speak English. The *American Benevolent Society,* 514–5465, tries to help visitors in financial difficulties.

Embassy consular sections will respond in cases of death or tangles with the law. The *U.S. Embassy* phone is 211–0042, the Canadian 533–0610, the British 514–3886.

 HOTELS. Within the national capital every possible type of hotel may be found; in the nearby cities the selection is somewhat more limited. Roadside motels are almost unknown. In this area there are no seasonal fluctuations in prices.

Mexico City

While Mexico City is big and spread out, most hotels are within walking distance of Reforma Boulevard (some, of course, are right on it) or of Avenidas Juarez and Madero, which are extensions of Reforma. Reforma-Juarez-Madero leads from Chapultepec Park to the Zocalo, the historic heart of the capital. The Zocalo is about three miles from the park. The Zona Rosa or Pink Zone is a trendy neighborhood on the south side of Reforma noted for its cafes, night spots, and boutiques.

Hotels classified as *Super Deluxe* at press time were authorized to charge up to $85 for a double room; *Deluxe,* $65; *First Class,* $35; *Moderate,* $20, and *Inexpensive,* $12.

Super Deluxe

Camino Real. Mariano Escobedo 700; 545–6960. An elegant prestige address near Reforma and the park. 700 rooms in a low rise spread out over 7½ acres. Four pools, tennis club, U.S. television, ten bars and restaurants including *Fouquet's de Paris.*

Maria Isabel Sheraton. Reforma 325; 211–0001. Next to the U.S. Embassy and across from the Pink Zone. With 850 rooms, this is Mexico City's largest hotel and a favorite convention venue. Rooftop pool, health club, U.S. television, seven bars and restaurants.

Nikko. Arquimedes 199; 203–0813. A Japanese-managed property with 750 rooms in a 38-story tower on the northern edge of Chapultepec Park with many Oriental and international touches.

Deluxe

Airport Holiday Inn. Boulevard Aeropuerto; 762–4088. 324 rooms, two restaurants, piano bar, and a delightful pool. Quite pleasant.

Airport Fiesta Americana. Boulevard Aeropuerto; 762–0199. New, with 270 large rooms, coffee shop, and excellent restaurant, plus entertainment evenings.

Aristos. Reforma 276; 211–0112. A Pink Zone favorite with 276 rooms, good restaurants, night club and disco. The location is ideal.

Century. Liverpool at Amberes; 584–7111; in the Pink Zone. New, small, with 142 rooms, luxurious bathrooms, small balconies, pool, sauna, restaurants, and night clubs.

Crowne Plaza Holiday Inn. Reforma 80; 566–7777. A Mexico City landmark, recently renovated, famed for its many bars and restaurants with some of the best nighttime entertainment in the city.

Galeria Plaza. Corner of Hamburgo and Varsovia; 211–0014. A 360-room Westin hotel in the Pink Zone. Exceptionally well run. Pool, two restaurants, piano bar, and disco.

Krystal. Liverpool 155; 211–0092. An attractive Pink Zone hotel with 355 rooms, in-house movies, pool, two restaurants, bars, and a nightclub.

Marco Polo. Amberes 27; 511–1839. Small and elegant, with a hot plate, wet bar, and U.S. television in all the attractively furnished rooms.

El Presidente Chapultepec. Campos Eliseos 218; 250–7700. 777-room highrise on the edge of the park, near Reforma and the Anthropology Museum. U.S. television. Half a dozen bars and restaurants including *Maxim's,* a disco and jazz bar.

El Presidente Internacional. Circuito Interior and Marina Nacional; 254–4400. One of Mexico City's newest hotels, a 400-room establishment built with traveling executives in mind. A bit out of the way for tourists. Pool and health club; next to big shopping mall.

First Class

Calinda Geneve. Londres 130; 211–0071. Pink Zone location. A 378-room Quality Inn originally opened in 1912 and recently refurbished. Excellent restaurant, pleasant garden bar and entertainment in the evenings.

Ciudad de México. Calle 16 de Septiembre 82; 510–4040. This converted department store is interesting; the *belle époque* lobby is a showplace; the restaurant and bar are quite good, but the rooms are shabby.

Emporio. Reforma 124; 566–7766. The location is good, the modernistic space age decor unusual. Most clients are Mexicans from the provinces. Coffee shop.

Plaza. Insurgentes Centro 149; 546–4540. An older establishment, with curious architecture, trying to make a comeback.

Plaza Florencia. Florencia 61; 533–6540. The 130 rooms are quite luxurious and the Pink Zone location convenient. Restaurant and bar with plenty more close by.

Reforma. Reforma and Paris; 546–9680. Once the smartest address in the city, now past its prime but reeking of nostalgic charm. Good location and old-fashioned service. Coffee shop, restaurant and show bar.

Royal. Amberes 78; 525–4850. Modern and attractive, with a nice restaurant, all in the heart of the Pink Zone.

Ritz. Madero 30; 518–1340. All 158 rooms are somewhat shabby and the financial district location is not the best, but the food is good and the bar fascinating.

Romano Diana. Mississippi and Lerma; 211–0109. A block from Reforma, this is a modern tourist hotel with a restaurant and bar where there is nightly entertainment.

Moderate

Del Angel. Lerma 154; 533–1032. "The poor man's **Maria Isabel**," with 100 rooms, is just across from one of the capital's posher hostelries. Reforma and the Pink Zone are a block away. Coffee shop, pool.

Brasilia. Avenida Cien Metros No. 4823; 587–8577. Close to the big Northern Bus Terminal; new, with 130 rooms.

Bristol. Plaza Nacaxa 17; 533–6060. Modern and pleasant, with 150 rooms, three or four blocks from Reforma and the Pink Zone. Coffee shop and cocktail lounge.

Corinto. Vallarta 24; 566–6555. Just a block from Reforma, this is a cozy 155-room hotel with a coffee shop and bar. Discount rates are available for extended stays.

De Cortes. Hidalgo 85; 585–0322; on Alemada Park a block from Juarez. Built in the 18th century, and with just 28 rooms, this is the smallest and oldest hotel in the city. Rooms face out on a colonial patio. Restaurant, bar.

Diplomatico. Insurgentes Sur 1105; 563–6066. A bit off by itself, but handy to the bullring and some of Mexico City's best restaurants.

El Ejecutivo. Viena 8; 566–6422. The 190 rooms are furnished with business travelers in mind. Near Reforma and the Pink Zone. Restaurant, bar, and pool.

Majestic. Madero 73; 521–8600. On the Zocalo, rather dreary at night, but in the heart of things during the day. The 80 rooms are well worn, but the rooftop dining is most pleasant.

Maria Cristina. Lerma 31; 546–9880. A charming old-fashioned Mexican inn with 110 rooms a block from Reforma, two from the Pink Zone. Garden restaurant, piano bar.

Metropol. Luis Moya 39; 510–8660. A commercial hotel with 165 rooms, just a block from Juarez, near the Alameda and Fine Arts Palace.

Prim. Versailles 46; 592–1609. Modern and attractive, with 160 rooms, nightly entertainment; close to Reforma and the Pink Zone.

Vasco de Quiroga. Londres 15; 546–2614. A 50-room gem in a residential neighborhood near Reforma and the Pink Zone. Good bar and restaurant.

Inexpensive

Edison. Edison 106; 566–0933. A 45-room hotel fairly near Reforma and a favorite with visitors planning long stays.

Fleming. Revillagigedo 35; 510–4530. A block from Juarez with 75 rooms and a restaurant. Modern with an inviting lobby and a fair restaurant.

Isabel. Isabel la Catolica 63; 518–1213. Downtown, near the Zocalo, with 74 rooms and old-fashioned Mexican surroundings.

Maria Angelos. Lerma 11; 545–6705. A favorite with repeat visitors not necessarily on a budget. The 20 rooms are shabby but homey atmosphere makes up for a lot. Dining room. A block from Reforma.

Monte Carlo. Uruguay 69; 585–1222. The glamourous name is misleading, but this downtown 59-room inn attracts many tourists on a budget.

Panuco. Ayuntamento 148; 585–1355. Near both Reforma and Juarez, unimpressive for outside but pleasant and cheap within.

Polanco. Edgar Allan Poe No. 8; 520–2085. Out of the way and rather Bohemian in a posh residential neighborhood.

Regente. Paris 9; 566–8933. Near Reforma, with 133 rooms, bar and restaurant. A favorite with budget tourists.

Del Valle. Independencia 35; 585–2399. A 50-room hotel a block from Juarez with a dining room and budget restaurants nearby.

Suites

For the price of a first-class room these establishments provide sleeping quarters, living room, kitchenette, and maid service. They are ideal for families and guests planning a long stay.

Amberes. Amberes 64; 518–3306. Small, with 28 units in the heart of the Pink Zone.

Junior Executive. Rhin 54; 566–3000. A block from Reforma, two from the Pink Zone, with 24 attractive kitchenette suites.

Mi Casa. General Prim 106; 566–6711. Close to Reforma, with 27 newly furnished units.

Orleans. Hamburgo 67; 533–6880. In the Pink Zone and handy to everything. The 41 units are attractively furnished.

Palacio Real. Napoles 62; 533–0535. With 30 units in the Pink Zone; restaurant and a rooftop piano bar.

Del Parque. Dakota 155; 536–1450. One of the few nice places to stay in the fashionable southern part of the city.

San Marcos. Rio Po 125; 533–6772. Near Reforma and the Pink Zone with 26 units (four to a floor), balconies, and marble baths.

Silver Suites. Sullivan 163; 566–7522. American owned with a bar and pleasant restaurant. Location, five blocks from Reforma is slightly inconvenient.

Motels

Most motels around Mexico City cater to romantics. Visitors who arrive by car usually prefer to park their vehicles and get around by taxi rather than wrestle with Mexico City traffic. The following are quite respectable, and prices are moderate.

Dawn. Highway 57 north of the city; 373–2155. Much like the Maria Barbara with restaurant, bar, and pool.

Maria Barbara. Highway 57 just north of the city; 397–4544. Pleasant rooms, restaurant, bar, and pool. Handy when arriving tired and late.

Parque Villa. Gomez Pedraza 68; 217–4637. In a residential neighborhood near Chapultepec Park. Garden setting and a most pleasant restaurant.

Cuernavaca

A favorite weekend retreat from Mexico City, Cuernavaca is some 2,000 feet lower in altitude, hence quite tropical. At first glance it is not especially attractive, but behind the walls the homes and hotels are beautiful. A double room in a *Deluxe* resort will run up to $80 per night; *First Class,* $60; *Moderate,* $40; and *Inexpensive,* $25.

Deluxe

Hacienda Cocoyoc. Yautepec (20 miles east of Cuernavaca); 12–2000. A 16th-century hacienda with 260 rooms (some with private pools) spread out over 70 acres. Facilities include nine holes of golf, riding horses, tennis, swimming, a disco, and a nightclub. Big with convention groups.

Hacienda Vista Hermosa. San José Vista Hermosa (about 15 miles south of town); 12–0300. Another 16th-century hacienda that is now a resort. Tennis, squash, and a large pool. Tour buses stop here for lunch and on weekends many people stop in just for the day.

Racquet Club. Francisco Villa 100; 12–2180. A Quality Royale inn with nine tennis courts and 36 marvelous rooms, all in a clublike setting on what was once a sumptuous retreat built for Nobel Prize winners.

First Class

Casino de la Selva. Avenida Gobernadores; 12–4700. On the edge of town, big and brassy with 228 rooms; cinema on the premises and a bowling alley, as well as riding horses, swimming pools, and a nightclub.

Las Mañanitas. Ricardo Linares 107; 12–4646. Better known for its magnificent garden restaurant, this establishment has 28 large and delightful rooms plus a big pool for guests only. Near downtown. No credit cards.

Las Quintas. Avenida Las Quintas 107; 12–8800. 45 units set around lovely gardens. Two pools, bar, and an excellent restaurant. A few minutes from downtown.

Jacarandas. Cuauhtemoc 805; 15–7777. The 90 terraced rooms look out over beautiful gardens and an inviting pool. Tennis, squash, and evening entertainment.

Posada de Xochiquetzal. Leyva 300; 12–0220. A 14-room inn built around a lovely garden and pool. The food is outstanding. Piano bar.

Hacienda de Cortes. Plaza Kennedy 70, Atlacomulco (five miles south of town); 15–9944. Lovely, small, with 20 units on the grounds of what supposedly was Hernan Cortes' hideaway. Pool, tennis, and golf nearby.

Moderate

Las Espadas. Rio Papaloapan at Rio Panuco; 15–3049. A garden resort, with a Jacuzzi, pool, and U.S. television. Nice restaurant.

Villa del Conquistador. Calzada Conquistador 134; 3–1055. Bungalows and cabañas set around a pool in a huge garden. Tennis, squash; restaurant and piano bar.

El Mirador. Francisco Villa; 15–1900. Cuernavaca's newest; large, with 100 rooms. Tennis, pool, restaurant.

Ancira Holiday. Paseo de Conquistador; 13–1010. A small 27-room inn with a panoramic view, heated pool, restaurant, and bar.

Inexpensive

Palacio. Calle Morrow 204; 12–0553. A downtown hotel with 16 rooms, restaurant and garden.

Papagayo. Motolinia 13; near downtown; 12–4694. Big with 90 rooms, a large pool plus restaurant and bar. Crowded with day-trippers on weekends.

OK Inn. Emiliano Zapata 825; 13–1270. A 46-room motel, some units with kitchenettes. Pool, restaurant. Tennis nearby.

Taxco

Perhaps 90 minutes south of Cuernavaca, Taxco can be either an overnight stop or an entire vacation. The choice of hotels is wide. The larger resorts are a bit out of town, while the smaller inns cling to narrow cobbled streets in town. The one *Deluxe* resort charges $85 for a double room; the *First-Class* places cost about $50; *Moderate,* $35; and *Inexpensive,* $20.

Deluxe

Hacienda del Solar. Highway 95 south of town; 2–0063. Intimate and quite exclusive, with 17 well-furnished rooms, tennis, riding horses, and pool. Outstanding restaurant with music in the evenings.

First Class

De la Borda. Cerro del Pedregal 21. Long a Taxco landmark, its 150 rooms looking out from a hillside over the town. Pool, nice restaurant, and entertainment nightly. Gets many bus tours en route to Acapulco.

Montetaxco. Lomas de Taxco; 2–1300. Quite splendid with 160 large rooms, in-house movies, and a magnificent view. Nine holes of golf, tennis, and riding horses. Mexican and international cuisine. Nightly entertainment.

Rancho Taxco Victoria. Carlos J. Nibbi 14; 2–0063. Under the same management as De la Borda but in town with 100 rooms. Classically Mexican with a lovely view. Two pools, restaurant, and bar.

Posada de la Misión. Cerro de la Misión 32; 2–0063. Close to town with 90 rooms laid out like a Mexican village. Pool and tennis; disco. The murals in the dining room are masterworks by Juan O'Gorman.

Moderate

Los Arcos. Juan Ruis de Alarcon 12; 2–1836. An in-town inn with 30 rooms, heated pool, restaurant, and entertainment evenings in the piano bar.

Loma Linda. Avenida Kennedy 52; 2–0206. A motel on the highway just below town with 90 units, pool, restaurant, and bar. Well-run but rather ordinary.

Inexpensive

Los Castillo. Juan Ruiz de Alarcon 3; 2–1396. The 15 rooms in this in-town inn are worth more than they cost. Small but delightful with bar and restaurant.

Sancta Prisca. Cena Obscuras 1; 2–0080. Also worth more than is charged, with 40 spacious rooms, colonial decor. The patio garden is lovely. Restaurant and bar.

Melendez. Cuauhtemoc 3; 2–0006. Just off the Zocalo, a 40-room commercial hotel, but quite nice and close to everything.

Pachuca

An easy day trip from Mexico City, Pachuca does not attract many overnight tourists. On the road there and beyond, however, are some interesting places to stop and pleasant places to stay.

Villa Arqueologica. San Juan de Teotihuacàn (en route from Mexico City to Pachuca); 511–1284. The famed Pyramids of Teotihuacan can be seen in a few hours, but stopping over is rewarding. Managed by Club Med, this hotel has 40 rooms, pool, tennis, and continental dining. About $35.

San Miguel Regla. Huasca (ten miles beyond Pachuca); 0–0053. A lovely 18th-century hacienda in the pine forests, now a 53–room resort with pool, riding horses, tennis, and putting green. Somewhat lonely except on weekends. About $40 with meals.

Emily. Plaza Independencia; 2–6617. A good downtown Pachuca hotel within walking distance of about all there is to see and a bargain at $15 per night.

Puebla

Although it is only a two-hour drive from Mexico City, Puebla is worth a one- or two-night stay. There is much to see and do and a good selection of hotels. A double in a *First-Class* establishment will cost $40; *Moderate,* $25; *Inexpensive,* $15.

First Class

Mision. Cinco Poniente 2514; 48–9600. The city's newest with 225 rooms, U.S. television, pool, three bars, restaurant, and evening entertainment.

Meson del Angel. Hermanos Serdan 807; 48–2100. A resort on the edge of the city with 190 rooms, tennis, bowling, restaurant, and bar. Entertainment evenings.

Villa Arqueologica. Dos Poniente 601, Cholula (about five miles from downtown Puebla); 47–1508. Adjacent to the Toltec ruins, run by Club Med with 40 rooms, pool, tennis, and an excellent dining room.

Moderate

Lastra. Calzada de los Fuertes 2633; 35–9755. Small, with 55 rooms on the edge of town, roof garden, pool, and good food.

Gilfer. Dos Oriente 11; 40–6611. A modern 90-room hotel downtown. Quite nice and close to everything. Restaurant, bar, and nightclub.

Palacio San Leonardo. Dos Oriente 211; 48–0555. Colonial in atmosphere with modern appointments. Rooftop pool, restaurant, and bar.

Posada San Pedro. Dos Oriente 202; 46–5077. Another charming downtown hotel with 80 rooms, restaurant, bar, and pool.

Royalty. Portal Hidalgo 8; 42–4740. With 46 rooms, many overlooking the Zocalo. Sidewalk cafe, restaurant, and bar.

Inexpensive

Cabrera. Diez Oriente6; 41–8625. Not very impressive from the outside, but the 60 rooms are clean and comfortable. Lobby and coffee shop are one flight up.

Palacio de Puebla. Dos Oriente 13; 41–2430. Close to the center of town. Adequate, but no restaurant.

Virrey de Mendoza. Tres Poniente 912; 42–3903. Cozy and friendly with just 18 rooms. No restaurant.

Agua Azul. Prolongación Once Sur and Calzada Mayorazgo; 43–1288. A working class resort with garden and pool. Crowded weekends but not bad the rest of the time.

Tehuacan

Mexico's most famous spa town is rather ghostly now. People do not take the waters as they once did. Still, Tehuacan has a special rundown charm. Rates are about the same as for hotels in Puebla.

First Class

Spa Peñafiel. Carretera Puebla; 2–0190. A rambling old resort that someone should turn into a movie set. Ample grounds, pool, tennis, bowling. Restaurant and bar.

Hotel México. Reforma and Independencia; 2–0019. A nice old place reminiscent of the German *bads*. The 50 rooms are well kept up and the dining room is good.

Inexpensive

Posada Tehuacan. Reforma Norte 211; 2–0491. A small, pleasant inn with home-style cooking, clean and comfortable rooms.

 SPECIAL EVENTS. January 17. Blessing of the animals *(Feast of St. Anthony)* with pets and working beasts decked out in their finery. Ceremonies at the Metropolitan Cathedral on the Zocalo and at other churches.
Mid-January. *Santa Prisca Fiesta* in Taxco honoring the town's patroness. Three days of outdoor dances by the Zocalo, fireworks, and general merrymaking.

February. *Pre-Lenten Carnaval* celebrated in a semipagan fashion at Teploztlán, roughly midway between Mexico City and Cuernavaca. Also, on a smaller scale in some Mexico City neighborhoods.

Easter Week. The *Passion of Christ* is reenacted in Ixtapalapa, a neighborhood in eastern Mexico City, beginning with the Last Supper on Thursday evening and going through a mock crucifixion on Friday. In Taxco the commemoration is even more impressive. Hooded penitents, black gowned and bare to the waist, flagellate themselves in an eerie candlelit procession through town.

May 1. *Labor Day.* Parade up Madero, Juarez and Reforma.

May 3. *Feast of the Holy Cross,* celebrated by construction workers as their day. Building sites are decorated with crosses and there is much exploding of fireworks.

May 5. In Puebla the *Battle of Puebla* is reënacted. It was in 1862 that Mexican forces successfully defended the city against the invading French. The month-long state fair gets started on this day.

July. On the weekend nearest the Fourth the American community marks U.S. independence with a fiesta of its own including a parade, patriotic speeches, carnival rides, food stalls and all the rest. At the American School.

Mid-August. Ten-day fiesta marking the Assumption, at Huamantla, Tlaxcala (between Mexico City and Puebla). Floral carpets made from petals and sawdust make this one of Mexico's most colorful fiestas. Also bullfights, charro rodeos, street dancing and fireworks.

August 13. *The Defense of Tlatelolco,* where the Aztecs fought their final battle, is marked by Indian dancing at the Plaza of the Three Cultures.

August 21. Tribute is paid to Cuauhtemoc, last of the Aztec rulers, at his statue on the intersection of Reforma and Insurgentes. Speeches and Indian dancing.

September 15. *Independence Eve* in Mexico City is another New Year's Eve, celebrations getting started at 11 P.M. when at the National Palace on the Zocalo the president rings the Liberty Bell, waves the flag and reënacts the original Cry of Liberty. Restaurants and night clubs stage grand and expensive celebrations.

September 16. *Independence Day.* Parade up Madero, Juarez, Reforma.

November 2. *Day of the Dead (All Souls' Day),* marked by the sale of special bread and candies. Candlelight vigil at the suburban Mixquic graveyard includes huge figures of skeletons.

November 20. *Revolution Day,* a national holiday, is marked by a spectacular parade of performing athletes down Madero, Juarez, and Reforma.

Last week in November. *Silver Fair* in Taxco with outdoor shows, dances, a beauty contest and, naturally, prizes to the Silver City's best silversmiths.

December 12. *Virgin of Guadalupe Day* brings pilgrims from throughout the country to the basilica to honor the Patroness of Mexico. Ceremonies start around midnight; crowds are huge.

December 16. The first *posada* and beginning of a Christmas season that lasts through Jan. 6, *Twelfth Night.* Yule lights go on and parties blast into full swing. *Posada* means inn and refers to the nightly search for shelter by Joseph and Mary; the search is reënacted at parties in many Mexico City hotels.

 HOW TO GET AROUND. Huge as it is, Mexico City is not difficult to negotiate. Much of what people want to see is within walking distance of the hotels, and when feet get weary taxis are cheap. For sightseeing, organized tours are the best bet. Visitors staying awhile will want to master the subway (Metro) and a couple of bus lines.

From the Airport. Taxis are available at both the domestic and international arrivals areas. These cabs charge about $5 to most hotels, much less than the gypsy cab touts try to steer tourists to. Rental car agencies have booths at both arrivals areas; however, unless you are heading out of town or know Mexico City very well, renting a car is not recommended.

Porters are available in the customs hall and just outside is a bank that will exchange dollars for pesos at the most favorable rate (better still, arrive with a couple of thousand pesos in notes and coins). The Mexico City tourist office and the Hotel Association bothhave stands in the arrivals area and will provide information and help the reservationless find a room.

By Taxi. Cabs come in many colors and sizes in Mexico City; the color and size will give you an idea of the fare. Large, unmarked cars with hooded meters are found outside the major hotels. These usually are driven by licensed English –speaking guides and may charge a minimum of $5 for a fairly short trip.

Red and white taxis operate out of stands, take radio calls and when picking up passengers on the street are authorized to charge a premium. Yellow and white cabs, often VW bugs with one front seat removed, cruise the streets looking for business. Meters no longer are readjusted to keep up with inflation; instead, new tariffs are pasted to a window advising if the meter says $2.50 the fare will be $1,000 (pesos). Often, however, passengers are told the meter is broken. Cabbies will quote fares in advance, which is fine if you speak Spanish. Yet, even if you are overcharged, the trip will cost less (or should) than a cab ride back home. Tips are not expected.

By Subway. While rising to compensate for inflation, Metro fares amount to just a few pennies, making a Mexico City subway ride the least expensive in the world. It is worth seeing, too, but avoid the rush hour. Between 10 A.M. and 4 P.M. the crowds are not too bad, but pickpockets are always a worry. Nice are the brightly lit marble and onyx stations, good signs, and the sleek French– designed trains that run on rubber tires. The Metro runs from 6 A.M. until midnight.

The various lines are indicated by color. Most used by tourists is the red line, Line 1, linking Reforma (Chaputepec station), the Pink Zone (Insurgentes station) and the Zocalo (Pino Suarez station).

By Bus. The fares are the same as on the Metro, and all the pickpockets not on the subway seem to be on the buses. In Mexican Spanish the word for bus and truck is the same: *camion.* In fact there is little difference between them. The only bus route of interest to most people runs along Reforma, Juarez and Madero from Chapultepec Park to the Zocalo. Stops are clearly indicated by attractive shelters and queues of waiting passengers. A bus also may be taken out Insurgentes Sur to San Angel and University City or out Insurgentes Norte to the Guadalupe Basilica. One can get anywhere in the city by bus; call 525–9380 for route directions. Trolley buses and trolley cars are found only in outlying areas.

Intercity bus tickets may be purchased at the Mexicorama office in the Plaza del Angel arcade which may be entered either from Londres or Hamburgo between Florencia and Amberes; 533–0298. Personnel speak English.

Buses depart from four outlying terminals: North, Avenida Cien Metros 4907; South, Tazqueña 1320; East, Zaragoza 200 and West, Rio Tacubaya and Sur 122. Subways run to all these terminals but passengers are not allowed to carry luggage on subways.

By Peseros. Painted green, these are cabs and vans operating on a fixed route, charging a flat rate (a peso once upon a time, hence the name) and cramming in as many passengers as they can hold. *Peseros* run along Reforma from Chapultepec Park to the Zocalo as well as along Insurgentes. There are many other routes as well, each with its own fare.

By Car. Millions of people drive around Mexico City every day and survive, but for out-of-towners the experience can be traumatic. Streets are confusing, traffic nightmarish and parking places almost nonexistent. Police tow trucks constantly are hauling away illegally parked vehicles; finding them takes fluency in Spanish plus many hours of hunting (call 658–1111 for clues on where to start looking). Visitors can hire a chauffeur for their cars for about $25 per day by calling *Drive Power* at 524–8512; many hotels also can arrange for drivers.

An automobile is the most comfortable way to reach such nearby communities as Cuernavaca, Taxco, Pachuca, Puebla and Tehuacan.

 TOURIST INFORMATION SERVICES. The Mexico City (Federal District) Tourist Office maintains information booths at both the international and domestic arrivals areas at the airport as well as on highways leading into the city. In town information is available in the lobby of the building at Amberes and Londres, in the Pink Zone. By telephone information is available from 8 A.M. to 8 P.M. by calling 525–9380.

The **Mexico City Chamber of Commerce,** Reforma 42 (phone 592–2677) publishes a variety of material distributed free to visitors. Open 10 A.M. to 2 P.M. and 4 to 6 P.M. weekdays.

In **Cuernavaca** the state tourist office is at the Borda Garden, Morelos 205; phone 2–1815. Open 10 A.M. to 2 P.M. daily except Sunday.

In **Taxco** information booths are located on both the northern and southern entrances to town on Highway 95, as well as in the Casa Borda a block from the Zocalo; phone 2–0979. Open 10 A.M. – 2 P.M. and 4 – 7 P.M. except Sundays.

In **Puebla** the tourist office is located at Reforma and Calle Siete Norte, phone 46–0928. Open 10 A.M. to 2 P.M. and 4 to 7 P.M.

 USEFUL ADDRESSES. *U.S. Embassy,* Reforma 305; 211–0042. Open 8:30 A.M. to 5:30 P.M. weekdays; closed for American and Mexican holidays. *Canadian Embassy,* Schiller 529; 254–3288. Open 9 A.M. to 5 P.M. weekdays; closed for Mexican and Canadian holidays. *British Embassy,* Lerma 71; 511–4880. Open 9:30 A.M. to 1 P.M. and 3:30 to 6 P.M.

The main Post Office is on the corner of Lazaro Cardenas and Tacuba; mail marked 'general delivery' *(lista de correos)*) may be picked up here. Near most hotels is the post office on the corner of Varsovia and Londres in the Pink Zone.

The *American British Cowdray Hospital* is at Observatorio and Sur 136; 515 8359.

Aeromexico has several ticket offices in the capital, with the main one at Reforma 445; 553–1577. *Mexicana* at Reforma and Amberes in the Pink Zone; 585–8933. *American* at Reforma 300; 399–9222. *Continental* at Reforma 325; 511–4988. *Pan American* at Reforma 35; 546–5715. *Western* at Reforma 381; 533–2000.

ENGLISH LANGUAGE MEDIA. *The News,* an excellent daily published in Mexico City, provides a good rundown on what is happening in Mexico and the rest of the world. It is available at hotel newsstands as well as at stands on the street in tourist areas.

Sanborns, which has three branches along Reforma and more elsewhere, is a good place to pick up U.S. newspapers and magazines as well as paperback books. The **American Book Store** at Madero 44, has even more.

U.S. network television is received by cable in Mexico City and many deluxe hotels offer this service. An increasing number of hotels have installed parabolic antennas which provide U.S. films, round-the-clock news and more. Radio VIP, which is FM, is Mexico's English-language station. It broadcasts CBS news on the hour. The station is the first on the left of the dial.

TOURS. There are more than three dozen tour operators in Mexico City running sightseeing excursions within the capital and its surrounding areas. They can arrange for trips anywhere else in the country as well. The better hotels all have travel desks that can set up tours. There also is *American Express* at Reforma 246; 563–2788; *Mexicorama,* Londres 161 (in the Del Angel arcade), 525–2346; *Mexico Travel Advisors (MTA),* Genova 30, 525–7520; *Linea Gris,* Londres 166, 533–1540, and *Turismo Del Paseo,* Reforma 185; 535–4408. Most tours are similar as are prices. Rates quoted here are per person in a bus; automobiles also are available at about $10 more per person.

City sightseeing. Includes the Zocalo, National Palace, Metropolitan Cathedral and Chapultepec Park; four hours, $10.

Pyramids. Takes in the Basilica of Guadalupe as well as a look at the major ruins at Teotihuacan; four hours, $12.

Pyramids plus Light and Sound. Similar to the above with the light and sound show added. Available only Oct. 15 through May 31; six hours, $14.

Ballet Folklorico, University City and Xochimilco. Available Sundays only, takes in a morning performance of the folkloric dances at the Palace of Fine Arts, goes on for a boat ride along the canals of Xochimilco's floating gardens, and continues to the modernistic campus of the National University; seven hours, $22.

Bullfights. Sundays only. Transportation to the bullring and back with a guide to explain the finer points of the spectacle. Four hours, $12. (Can also be combined with the Ballet Folklorico-Xochimilco tour.)

Night life. The best of these includes transfers by private car rather than bus, dinner at an elegant restaurant (frequently Del Lago), a drink and show at the Plaza Santa Cecelia where mariachis play, and a nightcap at Gitanerias, which features the best flamenco dancers in Mexico. Five hours, $50.

Cuernavaca and Taxco. Long considered the classic route with sightseeing in Cuernavaca and shopping in Taxco. Lunch is included. Twelve hours, $25. (Overnight stay in Taxco can be arranged for the price of a hotel room.)

Puebla and Cholula. Sightseeing in Puebla takes in the Cathedral and the Secret Convent; Cholula, a Toltec religious center, is the site of the world's largest pyramid (by volume, not by height). Lunch is included. Twelve hours, $25. (Overnight stays can also be arranged.)

Toluca Market. Fridays only, this trip is to one of the largest and most colorful Indian markets in the Mexico City area. Toluca is capital of the neighboring State of Mexico. The tour includes a stop at the Desert of the Lions, an attractive national park. $16.

 PARKS AND GARDENS. Chapultepec, spread out over 40 square miles on the western edge of the capital, is the world's largest metropolitan park. It also is the oldest park in the Americas, having been set aside as a reserve for Aztec nobility in 1435; they gave the place its name, which means Grasshopper Hill. Chapultepec has eight museums, three lakes, a zoo, and an amusement park. Also there are two good restaurants, several snack stands, theaters, the National Auditorium, and Los Pinos, official residence of the President of the Republic. Open until dark, Chapultepec always delights, but takes on a special festive air on weekends when scores of thousands of families come out to enjoy it.

Alameda, which means poplar grove (an *alamo* is a poplar tree), stretching from the Palace of Fine Arts over a four–block area along one side of Avenida Juarez, dates back to the 17th century. It was laid out by order of the viceroy, Luis de Velasco. The western corner is where heretics were put to death during the Inquisition. In the late 19th century the Alameda was where fashionable folk would stroll on a Sunday to see and be seen. Today the crowds are more bourgeoise, but the park remains every bit as lovely.

Xochimilco, the floating gardens, is part of the standard Sunday tour. Actually the gardens can be enjoyed any day. Visitors pile into gondolas and are poled along through the canals while boats bearing tacos and mariachi bands come by to sell their wares. It may sound too touristy, but foreigners always are vastly outnumbered by locals enjoying a day off. The gardens, by the way, no longer float. In Aztec times, when Mexico City was surrounded by a lake, rafts covered with soil were anchored out this way; flowers and vegetables were grown on the rafts. Today the rafts have disappeared but the vegetables and flowers are still grown in abundance out this way.

Desierto de los Leones translates into to Desert of the Lions which it is not. Rather, this cool pine forest was once owned by a family named Leon (Lion) who, since they never settled there, left the area deserted. Friday tours to the Toluca market often include a stop here to visit the remains of a Carmelite monestary built in the early 1600s. The park, less than ten miles from downtown, is a lovely place for a picnic.

Reino Aventura, on the southern edge of the city, is a theme park. The 100-acre spread encompasses six "villages": Mexican, French, Swiss, Polynesian, American, and Children's World. Admission fee ($3 at press time) includes most of the rides. There are also shows including performances by trained dolphins. And, of course, there a number of places to eat. The park is open 10 A.M. to 6 P.M. except Monday.

Cuernavaca

Borda Garden, by the Cathedral, was laid out along classic French lines by José de la Borda, a foremost 18th-century silver barron. In the 1860s, legend has it, the Emperor Maximilian would rendezvous in the shade of its great trees with a local girl who has gone down in history as La India Bonita. These days the garden is but a ghostly reminder of past glories.

Jardin Juarez or Juarez Garden, with its trees and benches, is an extension of Cuernavaca's main plaza. There are band concerts here Sunday nights.

Chapultepec, a smaller version of the Mexico City park, is more tropical and quite lovely, a favorite spot for family outings.

ZOOS. Chapultepec. Spread out over 60 acres, the park zoo is home for some 2,600 animals representing nearly 300 species. Most famous is the panda family; the two offspring are the only pandas known to have been born outside China. Another inhabitant is one of the first chimpanzees to return from outer space. The grounds include a children's area with a baby elephant, lion cubs, a llama, a donkey, turtle, and more. Youngsters can play with the animals, ride ponies, climb tree houses, and in general have a fine time. Smallers zoos are located in Pedregal and San Juan Aragon, outlying neighborhoods few tourists are likely to visit. The three Mexico City zoos are open from 8 A.M. until 6 P.M.; admission is free.

Puebla

Africam. Located some miles from town, but zebra-striped minibuses depart for Africam every 30 minutes. They arrive at 275 acres spread on the shores of Lake Valsequillo where 2,000 animals, some 500 species, roam free. Those driving in their own cars are urged to keep their windows rolled up. The few fences, which are scarcely noticible, prevent the lions and tigers from gobbling up the giraffes, zebras, and antelopes. Mornings and afternoons, the elephants put on a show. The park is open daily from 10 A.M. to 5 P.M.; admission at press time was $2.50 plus $1 more for those taking the minibus tour.

PARTICIPANT SPORTS. Golf. The five 18-hole courses around Mexico City are private but the better hotels can arrange guest privileges except on weekends. *Cuernavaca* has three 18-hole golf clubs open to the public on weekdays and the nearby *Hotel Hacienda Cocoyoc* has its own nine-hole course. Taxco's *Hotel Montetaxco* has a rather spectacular nine-hole course on a mountaintop.

Tennis. All the golf spots have tennis courts as well. Best bet, of course, is for players to stay at a hotel that has its own courts (see *Accommodations*). Or they can play at *Club Reyes,* just three blocks from Chapultepec Park, 7 A.M. to 9 P.M. (phone 277–2690 for reservations). In Cuernavaca the *Hacienda Temixco* has public tennis courts.

Swimming. Again, the best bet is to check into a hotel with a pool; all the golf spots also have swimming pools. In Cuernavaca the *Hacienda Temixco* and *Hacienda Real del Puente* both have several pools as well as restaurants and bars open to the public (neither is a hotel). In Puebla the *Spa Agua Azul* has a public pool.

Jogging. *Chapultepec Park* in Mexico City is crowded with runners early in the morning and *Alameda Park* gets its share as well (athletes should take into consideration the capital's 7,200-foot altitude). In Cuernavaca joggers will feel most at home at the *Racquet Club, Casino de la Selva* or *Hacienda Cocoyoc.* Puebla's Zocalo is another good place to run as is the *Hacienda San Miguel Regla* near Pachuca.

Cyclists and Rowers can ply their sport in *Chapultepec Park* where both bikes and boats may be rented.

Horseback riding is featured at several resort hotels outside Mexico City (see *Accommodations*). There are horses for rent at the Desert of the Lions National Park.

Mountain climbing expeditions up the Popocatépetl volcano with guides can be arranged through tour operators. The season is November through May and only experienced climbers need apply.

SPECTATOR SPORTS. Charreadas or *charro* rodeos are a Mexican original, true exhibitions of riding and roping skill. *Charros* are Mexican cowboys, although these days many are amateurs, wealthy executives and professional people who can afford the sport. *Charro* associations usually hold competitions on Sunday mornings to see who can most rapidly rope a calf or bring down a steer by its tale. Venues vary from week to week. Admission usually is free. Going with a guide is recommended in order to understand what is happening. One can, of course, go unaccompanied. Rodeos usually are held at the *Rancho del Charro,* Constituyentes 500 on the western edge of Chapultepec Park, or at the *Lienzo del Charro* in Pedregal in the southern part of town. Have your hotel call 277–8706 for time and information. There are also *charreadas* in Puebla.

Bullfights take place almost every Sunday at 4:30 P.M. in Mexico City's Plaza México. Easiest way to go is with a tour group so as not to worry about transportation or finding your seat in the world's largest bullring. Individuals may buy tickets (for as much as $10 for seats on the shady side) from hotel travel desks, or at the ring itself on the day of the event. The bullring is just off Insurgentes Sur about two miles south of Reforma and reached easily by bus or taxi.

Jai Alai is played every evening except Monday and Friday at the *Fronton México* on the Plaza de la Revolución just north of Reforma. The first game usually starts at 7 P.M. This is a Basque variety of handball with wicker basket-gloves enabling the ball to be hurled at tremendous speed. Betting on the outcome is as fast and furious as the game itself. Admission is about $1 and program notes explain, in English, what is going on.

Horse racing takes place at the *Hipodromo de las Americas* starting at 3:30 P.M. on Tuesday, Thursday and Friday, 2:30 on weekends. The admission price is minimal and you can place a bet for less than a dollar (or much more, if you wish). Extra nice is having lunch at the *Derby Club* (phone 557–4700 for reservations) while watching the races. Open throughout the year (except Christmas and Easter weeks), the track is a few miles north of Reforma, about a fifteen minute taxi ride from most hotels (buses run back to town).

Soccer is Mexico's most popular sport, some people claiming it was invented here in prehispanic times, transported to Europe and then brought back. Throughout most of the year games are played on Thursday evenings and Sunday noon at huge, 100,000-seat *Aztec Stadium* on the southern edge of the city, the *Olympic Stadium* in University City, or at the *Sports City Stadium* near the bullring.

Baseball is played almost every night and Sunday afternoon from April through August by the Tigers or Red Devils, the capital's two teams in the AAA Mexican League. Sometimes Americans on their way up, or on their way down, are to be found in the lineups. The games are at the *Social Security Park* on Avenida Cuauhtemoc, about a 15-minute taxi ride from Reforma.

Boxing and Wrestling matches are held Saturday evenings in one of two or three arenas around town. Although Mexico is the cradle of many champions, attending the matches is not recommended. The crowds are not very refined; often more punches are thrown in the stands than in the ring.

HISTORIC SITES. Great Temple of the Aztecs, by the Zocalo, was discovered in 1978 and fully excavated four years later. Actually this is the base of twin temples to the gods of war and rain. Both structures were reduced to rubble during the Spanish siege in 1521. Cortes ordered an Iberian-style city built over the site. During their digging, archaeologists found countless sculptures and artifacts, many of which are to be seen here. Open from 10 A.M. to 1 P.M. except Mondays. Brochures explaining the site in detail are on sale, but it is more rewarding to go with a guide; there are no guides at the temple itself.

National Palace, on the Zocalo, is almost next door to the Great Temple. Originally it was constructed on Cortes' orders using Aztec rubble, and since rebuilt and modified considerably, the third story having been added in the early 1900s. This was the official residence of the Spanish viceroys and now houses the offices of the President of the Republic and the Finance Ministry. The murals over the principal stairway are by Diego Rivera. The bell above the central balcony is the one rung in Dolores, Guanajuato, by Father Miguel Hidalgo in 1810 when he launched the War on Independence. Open daily from 8 A.M. until 6 P.M.

Metropolitan Cathedral, on the Zocalo, was begun in 1573 and completed two centuries later. This is the largest church in Mexico. Within are 16 chapels and 21 altars, not to mention a crypt containing 3,000 tombs. It is best to come with a guide who can point out the subtleties in the baroque and *churrigueresque* decor. Open daily until 8 P.M.

National Pawn Shop on the Zocalo is the headquarters of a federal institution with many branches. This 18th-century palace was turned into a pawnshop by the Count of Regla as a bank for the poor. It continues to serve as just that and within many pawned items are for sale. Closed on weekends.

Historic Center of the City. Much of the area around the Zocalo has been restored to its colonial splendor. In many ways it is a vast outdoor museum of the viceregal era when Mexico City was known as the City of Palaces. Public buildings, churches, and aristocratic mansions have been refurbished. The entire area covers more than 600 blocks.

Legislative Palace, about ten blocks east of the Zocalo at Corregodora and Morazan, is the equivalent of the capitol in Washington, D.C. Dedicated in 1981, it is state of the art in the lawmaking industry, a marvel of electronic gagetry and a monument to the days when Mexico was flush with oil riches. Closed weekends.

Hospital de Jesus, about three blocks south of the Zocalo at Pino Suarez and El Salvador, was the first hospital in Mexico. Buried within its chapel, almost unnoticed, lie the remains of Hernan Cortes.

Iturbide Palace, Madero between Boliva and Gante, west of the Zocalo, is a 17th-century residence that served as the imperial mansion of the first ruler of independent Mexico, Augustin de Iturbide, who styled himself Emperor Augustin I and ended up, like the next emperor, before a firing squad. Today the palace is a bank.

House of Tiles at Madero and Lazaro Cardenas on the western edge of the old city, is the most lavish of the 18th-century palaces. This was the metropolitan seat of the counts of Orizaba; today it houses the original Sanborns, a chain of upscale American-style drug stores. The restaurant in the now-roofed patio retains much of the mansion's original grandeur.

Monument of the Revolution. Beyond the House of Tiles, Madero becomes Avenida Juarez, which runs west 15 blocks to this 200 foot high monolithic domed monument. Originally this was to have been the Capitol or Legislative Palace. Construction was begun in 1910 by Porfirio Diaz to mark the centennial of Mexican Independence; Diaz had ruled Mexico for some 30 years. It was in 1910 that the Diaz regime was toppled and construction on the project stopped. In the end what was to have been testimonial to a dictatorship ended up as a memorial to its downfall.

Chapultepec Castle is another monument to fallen dreams. It was begun in 1785, designed to be a viceregal retreat, but never completed. By 1810 Mexico had declared its independence and in the years the followed the castle became the National Military Academy. In 1847 it was one of the last Mexican strongholds during the American invasion; a monument to the defenders, the Boy Heros, stands below the castle. Maximilian, during his brief reign, made the castle his imperial palace. Later it served as the home of several presidents, many of whom came to a sorry end. In 1940 Los Pinos was built nearby as the official residence of the nation's chief executives and all have fared better. The castle is open daily except Tuesday 9 A.M. to 5 P.M. There is a small entrance fee.

Plaza of the Three Cultures, Lazaro Cardenas and Flores Magón near Reforma Norte. This is in Tlatelolco where the Aztecs fought their final battle against the Spanish. Here are to be seen the ruins of an Aztec ceremonial center and, towering above it the fortress-like 16th-century Church of Santiago. Soaring over both is the gleaming white headquarters of the Mexican Foreign Ministry. Thus three cultures—pre-Hispanic, colonial, and contemporary—are represented at the plaza.

Basilica of Guadalupe. Calzada Misterios near Insurgentes Norte toward the northern edge of the city. This is the holiest shrine in Mexico. Here in Aztec times stood the Temple of Tonantzin, mother of the gods. Shortly after the conquest, in 1531, the Virgin Mary is said to have appeared before a recently converted Indian, one Juan Diego, requesting that a chapel be built on the site. To convice the skeptical bishop, the Virgin instructed Juan Diego to pluck some roses from the site and bring them to the cleric. The Indian did so, carrying the flowers in his tunic; when he opened the garment he and the bishop discovered a portrait of Mary painted on the cloth. That miraculous tunic, framed in gold, hangs over the white marble altar in the new basilica, dedicated in 1976. The new ultramodern basilica is an architectural marvel, although not everybody likes it. The old basilica, built in the 18th century, had been damaged in several earthquakes and was considered structurally unsafe. The old basilica replaced the original chapel built at the Virgin's request.

Teotihuacan

About 30 miles north of Mexico City, Teotihuacan, famed for its pyramids, was, some 1,500 years ago, perhaps the largest city on earth and capital of an empire that extended from the Texas border to Guatemala. It was a remarkably well planned metropolis extending over eight square miles. Sometime in the 8th century it was abandoned, probably following either an invasion or internal rebellion. The Aztecs believed it had been built as the gathering place of the gods. The site is open daily from 9 A.M. until 5 P.M. There is a small admission fee. English-speaking guides are available.

Pyramid of the Sun, nearly 2,000 years old, is the grandest and one of the most ancient structures at the site. It is 210 feet high and has been considerably reconstructed. The pyramid stands over a cave which, archaeologists theorize, the Tetotihuacanos believed to have been the center of the universe.

Pyramid of the Moon. Dominating a plaza surrounded by what are taken to have been shrines, this is a somewhat newer and more sophisticated structure. Pyramids in Mexico were built as a base for temples and apparently elaborate ceremonies were carried out on the steps leading to the temples. The Moon Pyramid has not been as completely restored as its neighbor.

The Avenue of the Dead, leading south from the Pyramid of the Moon, is misnamed. What once were taken to be tombs lining the street later turned out to be temples and priestly homes. This was the main boulevard and probably the marketplace for a city of 200,000. The avenue leads to a complex of shrines known as the *Citadel* and on to the *Temple of Quetzacoatl* (the Plummed Serpent God).

Acolman, on the road to Teotihuacan, is one of the monasteries built in Mexico. Dating from the early 16th century, it was built by the Augustinians and rather resembles a medieval castle. What makes it quite special is the fact that in the mid-1700s the monastery was flooded, half-buried in mud and abandoned. Since restored, it is something of a fossil depicting exactly the artful surroundings enjoyed by the brothers some 200 years ago. Acolman is open from 10 A.M. to 6 P.M. except on Friday; there is a small entrance fee.

Pachuca

Casa de Caja, downtown, was built in 1670 to hold "the king's fifth," the 20% of all silver mined that was paid into the Royal Treasury. So productive were the mines of the region that the Counts of Regla sent great amounts of silver to Rome to help pay for the construction of the Vatican.

Casa Colorado, downtown, is the Red House that was built in the late 1600s as the seat of the Counts of Regla.

Tula

Although it is in Hidalgo State, of which Pachuca is capital, Tula is most easily reached by Highway 57 which runs north from Mexico City to Queretaro. Here are to be found the ruins of what was the capital of the Toltec Empire. The once grand city was sacked and destroyed by raiding barbarian hordes in the 13th century and the site virtually unknown until archaeologists discovered it in 1938. Reconstructed since then is the Pyramid of Quetzacoatl topped with several 15-foot-high columns carved as warriors; these figures are some of the best known pre-Hispanic sculptures. The site attracts few visitors and has a feeling of eerie desolation. Open 8 A.M. until 6 P.M.; there is a small admission fee.

Cuernavaca

Palace of Cortes, on the Zocalo, is the city's most famous landmark. Construction of the building began in 1530 and while it no doubt has been modified over the centuries, the palace looks as old as it is. Once the seat of the Morelos state legislature, it now contains a museum. Especially worth seeing are the Diego Riviera murals within, commissioned by Dwight Morrow when he was U.S. Ambassador to Mexico. Open 10:30 A.M. to 6 P.M. daily except Sunday. Small admission charge.

Cathedral, Hidalgo and Morelos, was begun in 1525 and completed a quarter of a century later. The bell towers were built much later. Unlike most Mexican churches, the Cuernavaca Cathedral is almost starkly barren within. Once lavish, the building was frequently sacked during the rebellions and civil wars of the 19th century. Today the decor is stark and handsomely modern. One wall displays recently discovered murals depicting the martyrdom of 25 missionaries who sailed to Japan from what was then New Spain in the 16th century.

Teopanzolco Pyramid, at the end of Calle Rio Balsas near the railway station. An Aztec structure, this was a smaller version of the *Great Temple* in Mexico City. The remains of two shrines are to be seen at the top, one honoring the god of war, the other the god of rain. Open from 9 A.M. to 6 P.M. except Thursdays; small admission fee.

Xochicalo Ruins, about 30 miles southeast of the city, are fascinating, handsomely restored, and, for some reason, little visited. A city of perhaps 20,000, Xochicalco was inhabited from 200 B.C. to 1000 A.D. and may well have been the only center of civilization following the demise of Teotihuacan and the rise of the Toltec Empire and Tula. Baffling to archaeologists are the indications of a strong Maya influence so far from Yucatan and Central America. The site is open daily from 9 A.M. to 6 P.M.; small admission fee.

Taxco

Santa Prisca Church, on the Zocalo. A baroque classic, Santa Prisca was built at the behest of José de la Borda, a European adventurer who struck it rich in Taxco when he stumbled on a large vein of silver. In ordering the construction of the church he declared grandly, "God gives to Borda; Borda gives to God." Within are two of the finest paintings executed by Miguel Cabrera, one of the best Mexican artists of the colonial area.

Casa Figueroa, Guadalupe 2, is a colonial structure originally known as the House of Tears; a local official had it built using forced labor. It was restored to its former grandeur by an artist named Figueroa as a gallery to display his paintings. Open 10 A.M. to 1 P.M. and 3 to 7 P.M.; admission charge.

Casa Humboldt, Alarcon near Pineda, takes its name from the German traveler Alexander von Humboldt who sojourned there briefly in 1803. Moorish in design, this was once an inn used by those struggling between Acapulco and Mexico City. Today it contains a government run crafts shop. Open daily except Sunday during business hours.

Puebla

Cathedral. The most imposing structure in the city, the Cathedral, on the Zocalo, was completed in 1650 after 75 years of work. There are 14 chapels within. The high altar in onyx, marble, and gold, is the work of Manuel Tolsa, a master colonial architect.

Rosary Chapel, Church of Santo Domingo, Cinco de Mayo and Cuatro Poniente. Dazzling and splendid, a masterpiece in carved wood, gold leaf, marble and tile, the chapel was dedicated to the Virgin of the Rosary in 1690. Other religious art in Mexico pales in comparison.

Loreto and Guadalupe Forts, Avenida Ocho Norte on the outskirts of town, mark the spot where in 1862 Gen. Ignacio Zaragoza defeated a French expeditionary force. This was the only major victory ever won by Mexicans over a foreign army and the anniversary, May 5th *(Cinco de Mayo)* is still celebrated as a holiday.

Cholula Pyramid in Cholula, about five miles west of Puebla, is by sheer volume the largest pyramid in the world. Covering 45 acres, it resembles a grassy hill topped by a church. The Spaniards attempted to destroy this pagan structure, leaving only what they believed was earthen fill in its place. Actually a smaller pyramid—one still larger than the *Pyramid of the Moon* at Teotihuacan—lay buried within. In pre-Hispanic times new pyramids frequently were built over older ones. Visitors now can go through tunnels to the interior. Cholula was a great holy city in Aztec times. The Spaniards set about destroying its temples and replacing them with churches, giving rise to the story that the little town has a church for every day of the year. Actually, there are only 46 and most are in a sad state of disrepair. Near the pyramid itself is the *Patio of the Altars* with the remains of some fascinating paintings, including one picturing a drunken orgy that took place back in the second or third century. Open 10 A.M. to 5 P.M.; small admission charge.

 LIBRARIES. *The Benjamin Franklin Library* at Londres 16 (tel. 591–0244), near the Pink Zone and Reforma, is the closest thing in Mexico City to an American public library. Open Mondays through Fridays 10 A.M. to 6 P.M., it has an excellent reference section and a wide selection of current periodicals. Books are loaned only to residents. *The Anglo-Mexican Cultural Institute,* Antonio Caso 127 (tel. 566–6739), a few blocks north of Reforma, is similar but with a British orientation. The *American Chamber of Commerce,* Lucerna 78 (tel. 566–0866)), a block south of Reforma, has a small library of publications of interest to business people. Open weekdays 9 A.M. to 1 P.M. and 3 to 5 P.M. *The National Library of Anthropology and History* at Reforma and Gandhi in Chapultepec Park (tel. 288–0700), usually has an exhibit relating to the country's past. Open weekdays 9 A.M. to 6 P.M. *The National Archives* at Eduardo Molina and Albañiles (tel. 789–5915) near the Zocalo is interesting both for its exhibits and the fact that it is housed in what was Mexico City's most notorious prison. Open weekdays 10 A.M. to 6 P.M.

Puebla's Palafox Library on Cinco Oriente behind the Cathedral, is a shrine for bibliophiles. Within are some 50,000 volumes dating from the colonial period as well as globes and maps from that era. The library is in a 17th-century palace and is open 9 A.M. to 3 P.M. weekdays and 10 A.M. to 1 P.M. weekends.

 MUSEUMS. A visitor could go to one of Mexico City's museums every day for a month and not see all of them. The selection is enormous and there are more in the cities and towns surrounding the capital. In almost all cases admission charges, where they exist, are less than a dollar. Labels and explanations are, of course, in Spanish.

National Museum of Anthropology and History, on Reforma in Chapultepec Park, is perhaps the most outstanding institution of its kind in the world. Within is the Aztec Calendar Stone, unofficial symbol of the country, giant Olmec sculptured heads carved nearly 3,000 years ago in the steamy jungles of Veracruz' Gulf Coast, a replica of the painted temples of Bonampak (the original, in much worse condition, is in the wilds of Chiapas), along with treasures rescued from the Well of Sacrifice in Chichen Itza, Yucatan. The second floor contains ethnological displays depicting life as it is lived today in Mexico's more primitive villages. Multilingual guides are available. Open 10 A.M. to 7 P.M. except Mondays; entrance fee.

National Museum of History in Chapultepec Castle traces Mexico's past from the time of the conquest through the 1910 Revolution. Bringing the past to life are murals by José Climente Orozco, David Alfaro Siquieros, Juan O'Gorman and others. Especially interesting are the imperial apartments occupied by Maximilian and Carlota during their brief reign. The museum is open daily from 9 A.M. to 5 P.M.; entrance fee. Guides are available.

Gallery of Mexican History, near the Castle, contains a series of three-dimensional scenes out of the past including Father Hidalgo giving his Cry of Liberty and various battles. It is designed for school children, but worth a visit as it puts the country's history in focus. Admission is free.

Museum of Modern Art, on Reforma in the park, has a permanent exhibit of post-independence artists as well as temporary exhibits by both Mexican and foreign contemporaries. Entrance fee.

Rufino Tamayo Museum, Reforma and Gandhi in the park, is the newest in Mexico City. Built around a collection of works by Tamayo (considered the dean of Mexican modernists) and a permanent exhibition of 300 paintings from around the world, the institution usually also puts on the most exciting art shows in the capital. Open daily except Mondays 10 A.M. to 6 P.M.; entrance fee.

Museum of Fine Arts, Palace of Fine Arts by Alameda Park, Juarez and Lazaro Cardenas. The exhibition includes Diego Rivera's second version of his Rockefeller Center mural. The original was smashed because it contained a portrait of Lenin; in this one Rivera added Marx and Trotsky as well, along with an unflattering representation of old John D. There are usually some interesting temporary exhibits here as well. Open daily except Monday, 10:30 A.M. to 4:30 P.M.

National Art Museum, Tacuba 8, near Lazaro Cardenas and the Fine Arts Museum. Opened in 1983 in an elegant 19th-century ministry, this museum concentrates on works by Mexican artists from prehispanic times to the present. Previous visitors to the capital will recognize the equestrian piece outside as *El Caballito,* the Little Horse that stood for decades at the intersection of Juarez and Reforma. The horse carries Charles IV of Spain, but Mexicans studiously ignore His Majesty; indeed a plaque on the base explains the sculpture is shown not out of any love of royalty but because it is a work of art. A work of art it is, too, 30 tons of bronze that has been acclaimed as one of the finest equestrian works ever produced. It was sculpted by Manuel Tolsa in 1802. Open daily except Monday 10 A.M. to 6 P.M.; entrance fee.

Mexico City Museum, Pino Suarez at El Salvador (south of the Zocalo). Once the seat of the Counts of Santiago de Calimaya, this aristocratic mansion dates back to 1528, the walls built of rubble from Aztec palaces. It was considerably restored in the late 18th century. The exhibits within trace the history of Mexico City from pre-Hispanic times to the present. Open daily except Mondays 9 A.M. to 6 P.M. Free.

National Museum of Folk Art, Juarez 44, is one place where many of the exhibits are for sale. Shown are the best works by artisans from all over the country. Blown glass, copperware, pottery, and weavings are among the items fabricated the old-fashioned way that are on display. Open daily from 10 A.M. to 6 P.M. Free.

Polyforum, Insurgentes Sur and Filadelfia, stands by the towering, long unfinished Hotel de México. The area is surrounded by a violent, huge three-dimensional mural, "The March of Humanity," that was the final work by David Alfaro Siquieros. Within, there is an art gallery, theater, and dance hall as well as a display of fine handicrafts which may be purchased. Open daily 10 A.M. to 9 P.M. Free.

Carmelite Convent, Avenida Revolución in San Angel is a 17th-century nunnery with a notable collection of religious art from that era. Convents were numerous in colonial Mexico, serving as repositories for young ladies of breeding who could not come up with enough of a dowry to land a husband. Necrophiles will enjoy the crypt where the mummified remains of several priests and nuns are on display (the mummification was accidental and discovered only when tombs were opened during a construction project). Open daily except Mondays 10 A.M. to 5 P.M.; admission fee.

Museum of Intervention, Xicoténcatl and Viente de Agosto in Coyocan. Something of a Mexican original, this institution, housed in a former monastery, displays weapons, flags and other implements of war left behind by the various

foreign armies that have invaded Mexico. The site is where the Battle of Churu-
busco was fought during the Mexican–American War in 1847. Open 9 A.M. to
9 P.M. daily; entrance fee.

Mexico City Wax Museum, Londres 6, near the Pink Zone. Many famous
figures in Mexican and world history are brought nearly to life here. There are
a few Hollywood types as well, along with a chamber of horrors. The museum
is housed in a 19th-century Gothic mansion Charles Addams might have designed. Open daily 10 A.M. to 7 P.M. Entrance fee.

Cuernavaca

Cuauhnahuac Museum, Cortes Palace on the Zocalo. The building itself and
its Rivera murals (see *Historical Sites*) are more interesting than the actual
contents of the museum. The exhibits, which go from prehispanic times through
the Revolution, seem to have been gathered from attics and cellars. Cuauhnahuac is the original Aztec name of Cuernavaca; Cuernavaca (which means
'cow horn') is the Spanish version of the word. Open weekdays 11 A.M. to 6 P.M.,
weekends 11:30 A.M. to 7 P.M.; small entrance fee.

Museum of Herbal and Traditional Medicine, Matamoros 200. Herbal medicine has been used in Mexico since prehispanic times and still is preferred by
many country people. Herbalists are found selling their wares at most Mexican
markets. The museum exhibits some 60 medicinal plants and explains their
properties in a scientific manner. The house where it is located is fascinating,
too. It was built in 1865, supposedly on orders of the Emperor Maximilian who
installed here his mistress, the Cuernavaca native known to history as La India
Bonita. The museum is open daily from 10 A.M. to 6 P.M. Free.

Taxco

Sprating Museum, behind the Santa Prisca Church and one block from the
Zocalo. William Spratling arrived in Taxco from New Orleans, settled down
there to become the town's first silversmith. He gave birth to what is now the
community's leading industry. Much of his life was spent collecting prehispanic
artifacts and these are displayed in the museum, as are models of colonial mines
and how they were worked. Open daily 10 A.M. to 5 P.M.; small entrance fee.

Puebla

Secret Convent, Avenida Diezyocho Poniente 203, is a museum depicting
either devotion or fanaticism, depending how you and your guide see things. The
Reform Laws of 1857 outlawed convents and monasteries. In pious Puebla
many of the religious went underground until, during a fresh wave of persecu-
tion, three secret convents were discovered in Puebla alone (the government
today is more tolerant of these institutions). The Santa Monica Convent has
been opened as a museum. The entrance originally was hidden behind a cabinet
and the sisters attended mass while hiding behind grillwork in the wall. On view
are the cells in which they lived and the basement crypts in which many were
buried. Open daily 10 A.M. to 4 P.M.; Saturdays 10 A.M. to 2 P.M. Small admission
fee. English-speaking guides on the premises.

Santa Rosa Convent, Tres Norte and Catorce Poniente. Said to be where *móle
poblano* was invented, this is a shrine to Mexican cuisine. The convent itself no
longer is a religious institution, but the kitchen has been preserved. The tiles,
clay pots and stone stoves should fascinate gastrophiles. *Molé,* a spicy sauce with
a chocolate base, is Mexico's national dish. The convent is open daily from 10
A.M. to 5 P.M. and there is a shop next door. Free.

Alfeñique, Cuatro Oriente and Seis Norte. This is the state museum, but its interest lies primarily in the architecture of the building; *Alfeñique* translates roughly as "gingerbread," for as one observer had it, the structure seemed more the creation of a baker than an architect. The upper floors are maintained as they were when this was the home of local grandees. Open daily except Mondays 10 A.M. to 5 P.M.; small admission charge.

Bello Museum, Tres Poniente and Tres Sur. A motley collection of wonderful colonial paintings, tile artesanry (a Puebla specialty), colonial furniture plus iron locks and iron keys. Open daily 11 A.M. to 5 P.M. Free.

Pachuca

National Photographic Archives, Former Monastery of San Francisco, Calle Convento. The finest collection of photographic Mexicaniana is to be found here in the care of the National Institute of Anthropology and History. Pachuca was selected because its cool climate will not contribute to the deterioration of the photos. The old monastery itself is interesting. Built in the 1600s, two centuries later it was seized by the military and converted into a stable, then a slaughter-house, and finally a prison. Open weekdays 10 A.M. to 2 P.M. Free.

Tepotzotlan

Museum of the Viceregal Era, lies about 35 miles north of Mexico City just off Highway 57. A Jesuit church and monastery really comprise a small village founded around 1600. The former church is a masterwork in elaborate *chur-rigueresque.* The finest works of art done in the colonial period were created for the church and many of these treasures are to be seen at Tepotzotlan. Open daily except Mondays 11 A.M. to 6 P.M.; small admission charge.

 ART GALLERIES. The streets of Mexico City's Pink Zone are almost lined with galleries where works of art are for sale. *Estela Shapirio* at Varsovia 23; *Galeria Circulo,* Hamburgo 112; *Solaris,* Estrasburgo 19; *Tere Haas,* Genova 2; *Pecanis,* Hamburgo 103 and *Galeria de Arte* Mexicano, Milan 18, are among the most outstanding establishments. Also quite good are the art galleries in the hotels *Maria Isabel-Sheraton, Camino Real* and *El Presidente Chapultepec.* On Sunday at midday the *Art Garden* in Sullivan Park just north of Reforma displays work by budding hopefuls.

Cuernavaca's art shops are all one might expect at a weekend retreat for the wealthy. Best are *Galeria Akari* at Jardines de Tlaltenango 49, and *Van Gelder's* at Galeana 102. In Taxco there is a gallery run by the Fine Arts Institute on the premises of the *Montetaxco Hotel.* Puebla has its *Barrio de Artistas* or Artists' Quarter with outdoor exhibitions around the corner of Cuatro Oriente and Ocho Norte.

 STAGE. English-language theater understandably is limited in a Spanish-speaking country. An amateur group, *Theater Workshop,* puts on half a dozen programs throughout the year and they are quite good. Performances are weekends only at the Vasco de Quiroga Hotel, Londres 15 (tel. 546–2514).

Vaudeville is alive and thriving in Mexico City and language is not much of a barrier to enjoying it. The *Teatro Blanquita* at Lazaro Cardenas 16 (tel. 510–0751), a block or so east of Juarez, puts on two shows a day at 7 and 10

P.M. Mondays through Saturday with an extra 4 P.M. show on Sundays. Best seats in the house cost less than $5.

Visitors with a grasp of Spanish will find a wide choice of theatrical entertainment available, including translations of recent Broadway hits. Prices are quite low. Mexico City has no theater district as such; many of the best playhouses are a 15- to 30-minute taxi ride from most hotels.

Among Mexico City's top theaters are the *San Rafael* at Viginia Fabregas 40 (tel. 592–2954); *Manolo Fabregas* at Serapio Rendon 15 (tel. 556–1644); *Insurgentes,* at Insurgentes Sur 1537 (tel. 524–7871); *Julio Prieto,* Nicolas San Juan at Xola (tel. 543–3478); *Polyforum Siquieros,* Insurgentes Sur at Filadelfia (tel. 536–4521) and *Hidalgo,* Avenida Hidalgo 23 (tel. 512–0810).

MUSIC. The Palace of Fine Arts with its main auditorium and its Manuel Ponce concert hall is the center of classical musical activity in Mexico City. The Palace is at Juarez and Lazaro Cardenas (tel. 512–3333). Here the National Opera's seasons run from January through March and August through October. The *National Symphony Orchestra* has a spring and autumn season at the Palace.

The *Mexico City Philharmonic* presents several concerts throughout the year at the Ollin Yoliztli concert hall, Periferico Sur 1541 (tel. 655–3611). The *State of Mexico Symphony* gives performances at Nezahualcoyotl Hall in University City. Seasons vary from year to year.

The **Teatro de la Ciudad** at Donceles 36 (tel. 510–2197) downtown is the venue for a number of musical programs, both classical and popular, throughout the year.

The **Sala Chopin** at Alvaro Obregon (tel. 556–7411) presents a number of free musical entertainments evenings throughout the week.

Sundays at 1 P.M. there generally is a free concert at Chapultepec Castle.

In addition, on any given evening there are likely to be several musical events taking place in the city, and on Sundays there are several free presentations around town.

DANCE. The *Ballet Folklorico* performs at 9:30 A.M. and 9 P.M. on Sundays and at 6 and 9 P.M. on Wednesdays at the Palace of Fine Arts. The ballet, which has toured the world, is a stylized presentation of Mexican regional folkdances and is one of the most spectacular shows to be seen in Mexico. Hotels and travel agencies can arrange tickets.

The *National Dance Theater,* part of the National Auditorium complex in Chapultepec Park, and the Dance Center, Campos Eliseos 480 (tel. 520–2271) frequently put on dance programs. Other performances are listed in *The News.*

SHOPPING. One comes to Mexico City to see the sights, but one can very easily end up seeing mostly stores. Temptations are found at every turn, especially in the capital. The best the country has to offer is to be found here at ragged markets and glittering malls, in swank boutiques and peddled on the streets. There are more than a few tips to remember, however. The first is that "let the buyer beware" is the prevailing philosophy; selling plate and claiming it is sterling is considered shrewd business. Only the largest, most reputable establishments stand behind their products. Then, too, anything imported is likely to carry a staggeringly high price tag; duties in Mexico are hefty. Hotel shops as a rule charge more than their neighbors; they have to if they are to pay the rent. Tour guides almost always get a commission on anything their clients buy, hence they steer their people to whoever pays them the most. The Pink Zone is where most of the shops appealing to tourists are located, with many more along the Reforma-Juarez-Madero route running down to the Zocalo. The streets around the Zocalo downtown are a maze of little shops many visitors delight in discovering. San Angel, in the southern part of the city, is a colonial neighborhood with quite a sprinkling of elegant shops and boutiques. Polanco, just north of Chapultepec Park, is Mexico City's Upper East Side (northwest side in this case), address of many of the finest department stores and specialty shops. In the capital stores are open from 10 A.M. to 6 P.M. weekdays and until 8 P.M. on Saturdays. In the surrounding cities most shops close for lunch from 2 to 4 (sometimes from 1 to 5) and stay open later in the evening. Bargaining is an accepted practice almost everywhere but in department stores and supermarkets. Those who do not want to be blatant about it can ask what discount is available if they pay in cash or what exchange rate will be given for their dollars. In the markets haggling is expected, sellers often quoting twice the price they expect to get.

Handicrafts

Londres Market, Londres near Florencia, in the Pink Zone, is a typical neighborhood public market with one big difference. Many of the stalls sell a wide selection of crafts ranging from serapes and ponchos to baskets and pottery.

Centro Artesanal, San Juan Market, Ayuntamiento at Miranda, downtown. San Juan is a major wholesale produce market, its *Centro Artesanal* being a distribution center for baskets, leather goods, woolens, *piñatas* and the like. One can buy here retail as well, although the prices, even after dickering, are not especially low.

Ciudadela Market, Balderas at Plaza Ciudadela, about five blocks west of Juarez, specializes in handicrafts ranging from pottery and copperware to guitars. Prices are attractive as it is not too well known.

Fonart, Juarez 89. Other stores at Londres 136 and Insurgentes Sur 1630. Run by the government agency charged with promoting handicrafts, this chain of shops offers quality products at fixed prices.

Sanborns, Madero 4. Other stores at Reforma and Lafragua, by the Maria Isabel Sheraton and on Reforma across from the Chapultepec cinema, to mention but a few. The shop on Madero is the original, in the famed House of Tiles, and has a large, attractively priced selection of handicrafts.

Buenavista, Aldama at Degollado (take a taxi), is a virtual handicrafts warehouse, with a huge selection at wholesale prices. Open Sundays until 3.

Bazar Sabado, Plaza San Jacinto 11, San Angel, is open Saturdays only and worth staying over to visit. Only the highest calibre artisans are permitted to rent stalls here and almost everything imaginable in the line of crafts is available.

Indios Verdes, Acueducto 13 and Insurgentes Norte, on the northern edge of the city, is a way out, but has a huge selection and is open seven days a week.

Janus, Niza 20 in the Pink Zone, specializes in hand-loomed and hand-embroidered textiles along with paintings and sculptures.

Muller's, Londres at Florencia, Pink Zone. Onyx in all its glory is found here, from bookends and chessboards to tabletops. The store will handle shipping.

Silver and Jewelry

Los Castillo, Amberes 41 in the Pink Zone and Palmas 50, San Angel. Taxco silver at its best, much of it forged with copper and gold. An excellent place to buy special gifts.

Joyas de Plata, Copenhague 31, Pink Zone, also Taxco silver of exceptional style. Here the emphasis is on jewelry, fine stones set in silver. Many of the designs are inspired by pre-Hispanic art.

Paul Flato, Amberes 21, Pink Zone, features fine golden jewelry designed by the owner. Fancy stuff at fancy prices.

Tane, Amberes 70, Pink Zone. Jewelry and flatware in silver by a Taxco firm that now has shops in Houston and Palm Beach.

Mexican Opal Company, Hamburgo 203, is run by Japanese, who are very big on opals. Set and unset stones are available as well as a selection of jewelry in silver and gold.

Kimberly, Niza and Hamburgo, Pink Zone, is one of Mexico City's oldest and most respected jewelry shops.

Clothing

Girasol, Genova 39, Pink Zone, specializes in originally designed resortwear fashioned from hand-embroidered and hand-loomed cloth.

Aca Joe, Amberes 9, Pink Zone, began in Acapulco and now is everywhere. Sports clothes here are unisex, very mod and lots of fun.

Ruben Torres, Amberes 9, Pink Zone, has more sportswear from jerseys and jump suits to T shirts and shorts, all nicely designed and well made.

Ralph Lauren, Amberes 21, in the Pink Zone, is the home of Polo sports wear made in Mexico under license at Mexican prices.

Banana Republica, Florencia at Londres, Pink Zone, just the place to get outfitted for a safari to Chiapas or Texas.

Palacio de Hierro, Durango 230 (south of the Pink Zone) is the capital's most elegant department store. It specializes in labels signed by internationally known designers at Mexican prices.

Piña Colada, Leibnitz 11, across from the Hotel Camino Real, specializes in originally designed sports clothes for the family.

Leather

Aries, Florencia 14, Pink Zone, and Palmas 50, San Angel. An excellent assortment of shoes, bags, billfolds, belts, skirts jackets, and suits, all attractively fashioned. Many gift items as well. Prices are high.

Gucci, Hamburgo 136, Pink Zone. The name is a rip-off but the quality is excellent. Shoes, boots, luggage, and other attractive items made to demanding standards.

Ginatai, located at Niza 46 and at Londres 91, both in Pink Zone, specializes in boots and features custom made leather garments for both men and women as well as accessories

Castalia, Insurgentes Sur 318 (south of the Pink Zone) is a good place to find brief cases and hand bags at moderate prices.

Antil, Florencia 22, has a nice selection of leather clothing and accessories.

Or, Londres 157, in the Pink Zone, features suede and leather items for men and women.

Furnishings and Antiques

Lagunilla Market, Ecuador between Allende and Chile downtown, on Sundays is one vast garage sale. Not all the used tables and chairs are so old to be valuable, but many are.

Arte y Fauna, Copenhague 30, Pink Zone, is the local zoo housing fantastic animal sculptures by Sergio Bustamante. Worth a visit if only just to look.

La Granja, Bolivar 16, downtown, is Mexico's largest antique shop. To buy well one needs a discriminating eye and bargaining skills.

El Pabellon, Amberes 52, Pink Zone, is a small store filled with unusual furnishings and bric-a-brac.

Colonialart, Estocolmo 37, Pink Zone, is virtually a museum of antique furnishings and works of art. No bargains here.

Tamacani, Amberes 38, Pink Zone, is big with wall hangings and upholstry textiles. The looming is done by hand.

Artesanos de México, Amberes 61, Pink Zone, is a good place to buy traditional Mexican colonial furniture which can be made to order. They also have items in wrought iron and will arrange to ship.

Cuernavaca

The main shopping street is Avenida Guerrero, which runs off the main plaza. Along this avenue are to be found **Martha Bazar** with a nice selection of women's wear; **Artesanias Mexicanas** and **La China Poblana,** specializing in handicrafts, and **Casa Beltran,** a good place to shop for leather. Guerrero leads into the Cuernavaca market, one of the largest in Mexico. **Tianguis,** by the plaza, is a good place to find textiles and lacquered objects. **Ceramica Santa Maria** on Avenida Zapata, has several attractive lines of dishes and dinnerware. Modernistic religious art, some of it silver on wood and made by **Emaus,** is on sale at the Cuernavaca Cathedral. Best bargains in gifts are to be found at **Harry's Boutique** in the state penitentiary.

Taxco

This town of silversmiths is in reality a community of shopkeepers. Most are clustered around the Zocalo or the streets running into it, although a few good places are on Avenida Kennedy, which is what the main highway is called as it passes through town. **Los Castillo** and **Antonio Pineda** generally are recognized as having the best silver shops. **Emma** is quite good but not so expensive. All are around the Zocalo. **La Mina,** on Avenida Kennedy by the gas station, is a silver shop in an old silver mine and is fascinating. The **Spratling Workshop** south of town continues to turn out Spratling silver using the master's designs and molds. Handicrafts of all kinds are found at the **Casa Humboldt** by the plaza. Sunday is market day right on the plaza and this is a good time to hunt for huarache sandals, baskets of all kinds, leather goods, pottery, and wood carvings.

Puebla

Tile and other ceramics are Puebla's most famous products. The white and blue dinnerware used in good Mexican restaurants likely came from Puebla, as did the tile covering the domes of so many churches around the country. **La Purisma,** Cuatro Poniente 723; **Uriarte,** Cuatro Poniente 900, and **La Trinidad,** Viente Poniente 305, all are tile and ceramic factories that will arrange for shipping. **Talavera de Puebla,** in the centrally located Parian Market, is another good place to shop for tile. Onyx is another Puebla specialty and is sold is many shops. **El Parian** on the corner of Cuatro Oriente and Seis Norte is a good place to find low priced bowls, ashtrays and chess sets made of onyx. **Creart,** at Calle 16 de Septiembre 506, features an excellent assortment of handicrafts. Antiques also are plentiful in ancient Puebla. **Los Sapos** on Siete Oriente 401, and **Bazar del Sapo** on Plaza de los Sapos (a *sapo* is a toad) between Cinco Oriente and Siete Oriente, are good places to begin a treasure hunt.

RESTAURANTS. As befits the world's biggest metropolis, Mexico City offers a wide selection of restaurants, many of them outstanding. Hours are a bit later than in Anglo-Saxon lands and even in fast food joints service is never rushed. One can settle in for luncheon at a fine restaurant at 1 P.M. although it will be rather lonely until 2 and not crowded until 3. Stop in for dinner at 7 and some of the luncheon crowd may well be lingering over brandy (almost nowhere is the check presented until it is asked for). The fashionable hour for dinner is 9. There are American-style coffee shops (**Denny's, Vips, Toks** and others) all over the city and many of these never close. The Pink Zone has the greatest collection of restaurants. Insurgentes Sur, however, qualifies as Mexico City's restaurant row. San Angel in the southern part of the city, is noted for some outstanding places to eat as is Polanco, the fashionable neighborhood just north of Chapultepec Park. Reservations are a good idea in *Deluxe* and *Expensive* establishments. Jackets are required in these places and ties appreciated. Expect to pay $25 for a meal in a *Deluxe* restaurant, $20 in an *Expensive* place, $15 in a *Moderate* restaurant, and $10 or less in an *Inexpensive* cafe. Some of the capital's finest restaurants are open for breakfast and this offers a good way to try them while on a budget. Visa (V) and MasterCard (MC) are almost universally accepted, followed by American Express (AE), and Diners Club (D).

Mexican

Mexican food is much more than tacos and tortas, just as American food is more than hamburgers and hot dogs. Nor is Mexican food always hot and spicy. The country that gave the world vanilla, chocolate, turkey, tomato, and avocado has an extensive cuisine that will delight the most demanding gourmet.

Deluxe

San Angel Inn, Palmas 50, San Angel; 548–6746. Gracious living from the past is found at this restored mansion, a Mexico City landmark. The menu lists many international dishes, but the specialties include tortilla soup and pampano baked in maguey leaves. Open daily. V, MC, AE, D.

Hacienda de los Morales, Vasquez de Mella 525, Polanco; 540–3225. The manor house of a 17th-century hacienda, this is one of the capital's most elegant dining spots. International as well as Mexican dishes are served. Closed Sundays. V, MC, AE, D.

Expensive

Focolare, Hamburgo 87, Pink Zone; 511–2679. Regional specialties from Oaxaca, Veracruz, and Yucatán. Open for breakfast and famed for its mariachi brunches on Sunday mornings. V, MC, AE, D.

Hacienda de Tlalpan, Calzada de Tlalpan 4619 on the southern edge of the city; 573–9959. A wonderful place for a garden lunch or a romantic dinner (violins at night). International as well as Mexican fare. Open daily. V, MC, AE.

Nicolasa, Insurgentes Sur 1874; 524–1624. Mexican creole cooking served in an elegant 19th-century townhouse. The kitchen is highly regarded. Open daily for luncheon and dinner, for breakfast and luncheon on Sundays. V, MC, AE, D.

Fonda del Refugio, Liverpool 166, Pink Zone; 528–5823. Modest in appearance, gourmets regard this spot as a shrine to Mexican cooking. Closed Sundays. V, MC, AE, D.

Moderate

Meson de Caballo Bayo, Conscripto 360, near the racetrack; 589–3000. A huge ranch-style Mexican restaurant right out of the movies with strolling trios and mariachi bands. Lunches here have a way of going on until midnight. Open daily. V, MC, AE.

Fonda del Recuerdo, Bahia Las Palmas 39, north of Polanco; 545–1652. A large Veracruz-style seafood house where there always is a party going on. The musicians, too, are from Veracruz. Open daily. V, MC, AE, D.

Las Mercedes, Darwin 113 (near the Camino Real); 525–2099. Classic Mexican cuisine prepared to please gourmets.

Inexpensive

Beatriz, Varsovia 24, Pink Zone; 511–6054. Plain and simple, but with a reputation for serving the best tacos and tortas in town. A favorite with executives grabbing a quick snack. Open daily.

Cafe Tacuba, Tacuba 28, downtown; 518–4950. Open for breakfast, this is a marvelous spot to start the day or to drop in later for coffee and sweet rolls. Nice, too, for a light supper of hot chocolate and tamales. Open daily.

Las Casuelas, Colombia 69, downtown; 522–0689. Very Mexican, featuring all kinds of stews (which can be peppery) this is a good place for lunch when strolling through the old part of town. Open daily.

Circulo Sureste, Lucerna 12, a few blocks from Juarez and Reforma; 525–2704. Unimpressive, but regarded as the capital's best Yucatan-style restaurant. Open daily.

Spanish

There is surprisingly little similarity between the rather heavy cuisine of Spain and Mexico's lighter, more seasoned dishes. Mexicans, however, have a great fondness for Spanish food.

Deluxe

Centro Asturiano, Arquimedes 4; 203–2439. The dining room at this imposing Spanish social club is open to the public, serving truly authentic dishes yet noted as well for its Irish coffee. V, MC.

El Parador de José Luis, Niza 17, Pink Zone; 533–1840. The best and usually crowded with executives at lunch time, but quiet and romantic for dinner. Nice is ordering while enjoying a glass of sherry and a bit of Spanish torta in the bar. Closed Sundays. V, MC, AE, D.

Expensive

Meson del Cid, Humboldt 61, a few steps off Juarez; 512–7629. The decor is right out of Iberria and the medieval dinners Saturday evenings spectacular. Roast baby pig is a specialty. Closed Sundays. V, MC, AE, D.

Prendes, Calle 16 de Septiembre 10, downtown; 585–4199. A big barn of a place, Prendes has been packing in the crowds for nearly a century. Leon Trotsky had his last supper here. Hectic for lunch, relaxed for dinner. Open daily. V, MC, AE, D.

Moderate

Costa Dorada, Ejercito Nacional 648; 545–3086. Seafood in the Spanish (Catalonian, to be more specific) manner. *Pescado a la Sal,* fish baked in a thick salt crust, is a specialty. V, MC.

Lincoln Grill, Revillagigedo 24, a few blocks from Juarez; 510–1468. The name comes from the old Lincoln Hotel, but the restaurant is authentically

Spanish. An old standby, it shows its years, but the food is excellent. Breakfast served. Open daily. V, MC, AE, D.

Meson del Perro Andaluz, Copenhague 26, Pink Zone; 533–5306. A sidewalk cafe on a pedestrian mall, this *meson* attracts customers more for its setting than its food. *Moderate.* V, MC, AE, D.

Meson del Castellano, Bolivar 51, downtown; 510–8821. A good place to order *caldo gallego* and *fabada* in an authentic Spanish setting. Open daily. V, MC, D, CB.

El Vasco, Diezyseis de Septiembre 51, downtown; 513–0938. One flight up and a favorite with Basques who crowd in for lunch. Open daily. V, MC.

Argentine

South American steak houses are favorites throughout Mexico. Baby beef and churrasco is grilled right at the table.

Expensive

Rincón Gaucho, Copilco 3, just off Insurgentes Sur in the San Angel area; 548–3065. Run by an Argentine movie star who hit the big time in Mexico. Evening entertainment. Open daily. V, MC, AE, D.

Corrientes 3–4–8, Miguel Angel de Quevedo 401, toward San Angel; tel 554–8703. A good place for a late lunch or dinner with shows from 3 to 5 P.M. and midnight until 3 A.M. Big on atmosphere. Entertainment afternoons and evenings. Closed Sundays. V, MC, AE, D.

Moderate

El Fogón, Leibnitz at Darwin, Polanco area; 511–0814. Charming, with terrace dining a lunchtime, romantic indoor nooks evenings. Open daily. V, MC, AE.

La Mansion, Insurgentes Sur 778; 520–0202. Mexico City's original Argentine steak house remains a favorite. Indoor and outdoor dining. Open daily. MC, AE, D.

La Troje, Insurgentes Sur 1217; 598–4739. Argentine fare served country style. Piano music in the evenings. Open daily. V, MC, AE, D.

British

The hearty fare and clubby ambience of Great Britain's drinking and dining establishments are much prized and much imitated in Mexico City.

Deluxe

Sir Winston Churchill, Avila Camacho 67 (Periferico), Polanco; 520–0065. A rare Tudor mansion, wainscoted and regal within. Roast beef and meat pies are better than in the Old Country. Closed Sundays. V, MC, AE, D.

Expensive

Piccadilly Pub, Copenhague 23, Pink Zone; 514–1515. Both a sidewalk cafe and indoor restaurant, a big of England as it should be. Lager is served by the yard. Closed Sundays. V, MC, AE, D.

Sir Mark, Ameyalco 10, just off Insurgentes Sur; 687–1373. Descended from a restaurant founded by Sir Mark Hylesford, this is a British-run establishment, Victorian and elegant in decor. The lamb is excellent. Closed Sundays. V, MC, AE, D.

Calesa de Londres, Londres 102; Pink Zone; 533–6625. Classic, in a turn-of-the-century town house, with an English bar and English chops and roasts. Open daily. V, MC, AE, D.

Lancers, Insurgentes Sur 2018; 548–8736. Scots rather than English is this attractive establishment (the best British beef is from Scotland). Open daily. V, MC, AE, D.

Cochera del Bentley, Insurgentes Sur 1650; 534–8474. Open for breakfast, when it is especially nice. Organ music evening. Open daily. V, MC, AE.

King's Pub, Arquimedes 31, Polanco; 254–2655. An American-style English pub run by a former Mexican ad man. Most convivial. Piano music in the evening. Mexican buffet Sundays. Open daily. V, MC, AE, D.

French

Deluxe

Fouquet's, Hotel Camino Real, Mariano Escobedo 700, Polanco area; 545–6960. The only branch of the famed Parisienne restaurant, and in many ways the best restaurant in Mexico City. Romantic dance music at night. Closed Sundays. V, MC, AE, D.

Maxim's, Hotel El Presidente Chapultepec, Campos Eliseos 218, Polanco; 254–0033. A licensed replica of the Paris original with an outstanding menu to match the decor. Closed Sundays. V, MC, AE, D.

Del Lago, Chapultepec Park; 515–9585. Considered by many the most beautiful restaurant in the capital. Excellent kitchen. Quiet dance music in the evening. Closed Sundays. V, MC, AE, D.

Expensive

Rivoli, Hamburgo 123, Pink Zone; 525–6862. Established in 1953 by Dario Borzani and now managed by his son, the Rivoli is a gourmet landmark. Closed Sundays. V, MC, AE, D.

La Petite France, Presidente Mazaryk 360; 531–6783. Attractive and casually elegant, with a limited but excellent menu in one of the capital's most fashionable neighborhoods.

Champs Elysees, Reforma and Amberes, Pink Zone; 514–0450. Where real men eat quiche. Extremely fashionable and usually crowded (less so at night). Closed weekends. V, MC, AE, D.

Passy, Amberes 10, Pink Zone; 511–0257. Another fashionable meeting place, the main dining room overlooking an enclosed terrace. More relaxed at night. Closed Sundays. V, MC, D.

Villa Lorraine, Insurgentes Sur 1759; 524–5949. The elegant former home of the Papal Nuncio, noted for its desserts. Open for breakfast daily. V, MC, AE.

Moderate

Estoril, Genova 75, Pink Zone; 511–3421. The management is French, the ambience exclusive and sophisticated. Crowded at lunch. Closed Sundays. V, MC, AE, D.

Toulouse-Lautrec, Genova 74 (arcade), Pink Zone; 533–4786. An informal bistro with an especially appealing bar. Relaxed, pleasant service. Open daily. V, MC, AE, D, CB.

La Casserole, Insurgentes Sur 1880; 524–7190. Provencal country dining. A good place for snails. Open daily; lunch only on Sundays. V, MC, AE, D.

Italian

Expensive

La Pergola, Genova and Londres, Pink Zone; 511–3049. Nicely appointed, a favorite for business lunches. Romantic at night. Closed Sundays. V, MC, AE, D.

La Scala, Periferico Sur and Insurgentes Sur on the southern edge of the city; 573–6974. A show place with live music for dancing in the evenings. Closed Sundays. V, MC, AE, D.

Mediterráneo, Palmas 210, Polanco area; 520–8244. Dishes from many Mediterranean countries are served here, but Italian cuisine is the specialty. Nice for breakfast. Open daily. V, MC, AE, D.

Moderate

La Gondola, Genova 21, Pink Zone; 511–6908. One of Mexico City's first Italian restaurants. Attractive decor and excellent pasta. Closed Sundays. V, MC, AE, D.

Alfredo, Genova 74 (arcade), Pink Zone; 511–3864. Alfredo Conti, a Sicilian, is the owner and chief cook and host. His place is very popular. Open daily. V, MC, AE, D.

Da Raffaello, Londres 165, Pink Zone; 525–6585. A two-story delight, especially cozy in the evening. Good pasta and friendly service. V, MC, AE.

European

Deluxe

Mazurka, Nueva York 150 near Insurgentes Sur; 523–8811. One of the finest Polish restaurants anywhere and worth a special trip. A chamber music quartet plays at night. Open daily. V, MC, AE, D.

Expensive

Paprika, Chipancingo 16, near Insurgentes Sur; 574–2856. The capital's only Hungarian restaurant, and a good one. Closed Sundays. V, MC, AE, D.

Piccolo Suizo, Mariano Escobedo 539, Polanco area; 531–1298. Swiss owned, featuring a number of international dishes; boullabaisse on Fridays. Open daily (lunch only on Sundays). V, MC, AE.

Bellinghausen, Londres 96, Pink Zone; 511–1096. A big, masculine German restaurant with a beer garden in back. Jammed at lunch. Open daily. V, MC, AE.

Moderate

Chalet Suizo, Niza 37, Pink Zone; 511–7529. The specialty at this long-time favorite is cheese fondue. Open daily. V, MC, AE, D.

Sep's, Insurgentes and Paris, a few blocks north of Reforma; 511–0012. Alsatian cooking, beginning with rich pates and sauerkraut, is featured. Open daily. V, MC, AE, D.

Konditori, Genova 61, Pink Zone; 511–1589. Indoor-outdoor snacking at a Danish-style cafe. Good breakfasts and light lunches. Open daily. V, MC.

American

Deluxe

Delmonico's, Londres 87; Pink Zone. A show place established by Nick Noyes in 1954. Roast beef, excellent steaks and seafood. Wonderful breakfasts. Open daily. V, MC, AE, D.

Villa Reforma, Reforma 2210, west of the park; 596–0123. In an elegant residential neighborhood. Attractive glass covered terrace. Sumptuous breakfasts. Open daily. V, MC, AE, D.

Les Moustaches, Rio Sena 88, near Reforma and Pink Zone; 533–3390. New Orleans creole cuisine in a lovely but snobbish setting. Closed Sundays. V, MC, AE, D.

Expensive

Carlos Anderson's, Reforma at Oxford; 511–5187. Flagship of the country's best and largest restaurant organization. Zany, friendly, but with good food. Open daily. V, MC, AE, D.

Moderate

Shirley's, Londres 102, Pink Zone; 584–7111. Hamburgers, french fries, malts, and banana splits for the homesick. Open daily.

Oriental

Deluxe

Mauna Loa, San Jeronimo 240 in the south of the city; 548–6884. A Polynesian delight with Cantonese and Mandarin dishes. Hula dancers entertain at night. Open daily. V, MC, AE, D.

Suntory, Torres Adalide 14, just off Insurgentes Sur; 536–7754. One of the seven Suntory restaurants in the world, serving traditional Japanese dishes with flair and elegance. Closed Sundays. V, MC, AE, D.

Moderate

Luau, Niza 38, Pink Zone; 533–6058. A longtime favorite with lovers of Cantonese food. Open daily. V, MC, AE.

Mikado, Reforma at Guadalquivir, an authentic Japanese cafe just a block or so from the Japanese Embassy. Closed Sundays. V, MC.

Inexpensive

Yi-Yen, Hamburgo 140, Pink Zone; 528–6966. A pleasant, unassuming Cantonese restaurant. Closed Sundays. V, MC.

CUERNAVACA

Deluxe

Las Mañanitas, Ricardo Linares 107; 12–4646. A splendid garden is the setting for one of the country's top restaurants. The international menu includes Mexican specialties. Open daily.

Expensive

Chateau Rene, Atzingo 11; 13–1201. Country dining in the European manner. One of the best. Open daily. V, MC.

Sumiya, in Juitepec; 15–3055. The Japanese palace built for Barbara Hutton is a magnificent place to see. The food is international, with a few Oriental items on the menu. Open daily. MC, V, AE, D.

Moderate

Harry's Grill, Gutenberg 3; 12–7679. A happy-go-lucky Carlos Anderson place on the main plaza. Closed Mondays. V, MC, AE, D.

La India Bonita, Morrow 6; 12–1266. Modest, but easily the best place in town for Mexican food.

Vienes, Lerdo de Tejada at Comonfort; 12–0217. The menu is Austro-German, and the pastries some of the best found anywhere in Mexico. Closed Tuesdays. V, MC.

TAXCO

Expensive

Ventana de Taxco, Highway 95 south of town; 2–1300. Spectacular view (the name means "Window on Taxco") and fine North Italy cuisine. Open daily. V, MC, AE, D.

Moderate

Señor Costilla, Plaza Borda; 2–3215. Ribs, chops and Mexican specialties in one of Anderson's zany places. Open daily. V, MC, AE, D, CB.

Arnoldo, Plaza de los Gallos; 2–1272. Good, hearty fare in handy spot. Open daily, breakfast through dinner. V, MC, AE.

Celito Lindo, Plaza Borda; 2–0603. A charming little place with Mexican and international dishes. Open for breakfast.

Inexpensive

Bora Bora Pizza, overlooking the zócalo, one flight up. Oddly named, but a wonderful spot to watch the action on the plaza.

PUEBLA

Moderate

Max Internacional, Juarez 2915; 48–9503. One of Puebla's more attractive restaurants featuring international cuisine. Closed Mondays. V, MC.

Charlie's China Poblana, Juarez 1918; 46–3184. The best of Anderson's several establishments in Puebla. Closed Mondays. V, MC, AE, D.

D'Armandos, Juarez 2105; 41–8161. An attractive continental cafe serving local specialties as well. Open daily. V, MC, AE, D.

Fonda Santa Clara, Tres Poniente 307; 42–2659. Top spot for molé poblano and other regional dishes. Open daily. MC, AE, D.

 NIGHTLIFE. The emphasis is on night when it comes to nightlife in Mexico City. People meet for cocktails at 7 or 8 P.M., take in a dinner and show at 10 or 11 P.M., stop in for a bit of disco dancing at midnight and then find a spot for a nightcap at 3 A.M. The easy way to do this is on a night club tour (such tours sound unsophisticated, but they take in the best places and there is never any hassle over reservations or getting a good table, nor any worry about how much to tip). Those who want to go out on their own should have no trouble getting around; waiters will arrange for taxis to be summoned. The big hotels offer the best selection when it comes to night life; they are where most of the locals head. Outside the hotels the Pink Zone, Reforma-Juarez and Insurgentes Sur have the greatest concentration of night spots. Liquor, it should be remembered, packs a heavy wallop at the capital's 7,000 foot altitude but drunkeness is considered bad form. Imported booze is staggeringly expensive. Mexico City is probably safer after dark than most other towns, but muggings are not unknown. Going out bejeweled or flashing a wad is asking for trouble. Unescorted women no longer are considered shocking, but they may be subjected to attentions they do not want.

Bars with Entertainment

Lobby Bar, Hotel Maria Isabel-Sheraton, Reforma 325. Open from noon to midnight with mariachis playing from 7 to 10 P.M. Something of a refined singles scene.

Lobby Bar, Hotel El Presidente Chapultepec, Campos Eliseos 218, Polanco. Various musical groups perform throughout the day from 1 until 11 P.M. Quite crowded early in the evening.

Lobby Bar, Hotel Camino Real, Mariano Escobedo 700, Polanco area. Open noon to 10 P.M., with piano music early in the evening. Meeting place for the capital's elite.

Ritz Bar, Hotel Ritz, Madero 30, open noon until 10 P.M. with piano entertainment evenings except weekends. A favorite with bankers and politicians.

Karisma, Campos Eliseos 219, Polanco. A cozy place where couples meet after a hard day at the office. The music is romantic.

Show Lounges

The entertainment is the draw at these spots, most of which are pleasant either before or after dinner.

Caballo Negro, Crowne Plaza, Reforma 80; 566–7777. Continuous entertainment until 1 A.M. Closed Sundays. Cover charge $2.

77, Londres 77; 518–3539. A Pink Zone dive where the entertainment is sexy.

JB, corner of Londres and Niza, Pink Zone, 211–0112. Beer is served by the yard and the music is rock or jazz.

Guernica, Hotel Krystal, Liverpool and Amberes, Pink Zone; 211–0092. Imaginative and fashionable. Cover $2. Open 7 P.M. to 1 A.M. except Sundays.

La Mancha, Hotel Aristos, Reforma 276; 211–0112. Mariachis and other Mexican musicians play from 6 P.M. until after midnight. Cover charge $2.

Parjaro Loco, Hamburgo 188, Pink Zone; 511–9770. Part of *El Señorial,* a complex of night spots, this one a favorite of well-heeled youth. Cover $3.50. Open 7 P.M. to 3 A.M. except Sundays.

Feeling, Hotel Century, Liverpool 152, Pink Zone; 584–7111. A lively penthouse hotspot open from 8 P.M. until 2 A.M. except Sundays. No cover, no minimum.

Gatsby's, Hotel El Presidente Chapultepec, Campos Eliseos 218. Polanco; 250–7700. The city's best jazz bar swings from 7 P.M. until 3 A.M. except Sundays. Cover $4.

Dinner and Show

La Veranda, Hotel Maria Isabel Sheraton, Reforma 325; 211–0001. A top supper club, often with international performers, plus a dance floor. Shows at 10 P.M. and midnight except Sundays. Cover varies.

Regine, Hotel Century, Londres at Amberes; 584–7111. Strolling violins, elegant surroundings, a rooftop view, and passable food.

Casablanca, Florencia 36, Pink Zone; 525–2020. Part of the Marrakesh night spot complex. Dinner and dancing with a big, splashy show at midnight. Closed Sundays. Minimum $25.

El Patio. Atenas 9; 535–3904. A classic old-style nightclub with tiny tables, surly waiters, and miserable food; the place to see such headliners as Julio Iglesias and Vicki Carr.

Salon Luz, Leibnitz 14, Polanco area; 545–2562. Good Teutonic food. Shows twice a night except Sundays. Minimum $15.

Stelaris, Hotel Crowne Plaza, Reforma 80; 566–7777. Top names usually perform at midnight except Sundays. Good food and music for dancing. Minimum $25.

Plaza Santa Cecilia, Callejon de la Amargura 30, near Juarez; 526–2455. Typically Mexican and a standard stop on night life tours. Close to Plaza Garibaldi where mariachi bands congregate, the show here is all regional dances and folklore. Open until 3 A.M. except Sundays. Cover $3.

El Gran Caruso, Londres 25, edge of Pink Zone; 546–1199. If you can't find your waiter, he may be up front singing a Verdi aria. Dinner show at 11 P.M. except Sundays.

Maquiavelo, Hotel Krystal, Pink Zone; 211–0092. Mexican headliners perform at 11 P.M. and 1 A.M. nightly except Sundays. Cover varies according to the show.

Carrousel, Niaza and Hamburgo, Pink Zone; 528–8764. The entertainment starts early, keeps going, with music for dancing.

Discos

Lipstick, Hotel Aristos, Reforma 274; 211–0112. Longtime favorite where the fun starts nightly about 10 P.M. Cover $5.

Valentino's, Florencia 36; Pink Zone; 525–2020. Part of the Marrakesh complex. The emphasis here is on romantic music and touch dancing. Open 9 P.M. until 4 A.M. except Sundays. Cover $5.

Cero Cero, Hotel Camino Real, Mariano Escobedo 700, Polanco area; 545–6560. Live music as well as records. Bright lights and loud sounds. Open nightly 9 P.M. to 4 A.M. Cover $4.

News, San Jerónimo 252, in San Angel; 548–1636. Way out on the southern edge of the city but also very *in.* Nice after dinner at the *Mauna Loa* next door.

Gay Disco, Hamburgo 41, Pink Zone area. The name says it all. Open Sundays. No cover.

Disco Club, El Presidente Chapultepec, Campos Eliseos 218, Polanco; 250–7700. Recently renovated with a new sound system. Very popular. Open 9 P.M. to 3 A.M. except Mondays. Cover $5.

Le Chic, Hotel Galeria Plaza, Hamburgo at Varsovia, Pink Zone; 211–0014. Small, elegant, with stuffed chairs and modern sounds that deafen only the dancers. Open 9 P.M. to 3 A.M. except Sundays. Cover $5.

Late Night

Gitanerias, Oaxaca 15, just south of the Pink Zone; 511–1762. Flamenco dancing that does not get started until after midnight, goes on until nearly 4 A.M. Closed Sundays. Cover $2.50.

Afro Tramonto, Insurgentes and Sullivan (north side of Reforma); 546–8807. Rather wicked but not too rowdy. Appeals to gentlemen alone, but escorted ladies are welcome. Open from 10 P.M. to 4 A.M. except Sundays. Cover $2.

Guadalajara de Noche, Plaza Garibaldi (east of Juarez); 526–5521. A mariachi hangout that is the traditional last stop after an evening's revels. Open nightly until 4 A.M.

Cuernavaca

Action after dark in Cuernavaca is pretty much limited to discos which are usually open only over the weekends. Among the best are **Barba Azul** at Prado 10 (tel. 12–3255) which opens at 10 P.M. with a $2 cover; **Kaova,** Leyva 5 (tel. 14–3547), open at 9 P.M. but admitting couples only at $2 per person, and **Maximiliano's,** Juan Ruiz de Alarcon 7 (tel. 4–3547) with a $3 cover. The **Hotel Casino de la Selva** has a nightclub as does the **Hacienda de Cocoyoc,** but the latter is 30 minutes out of town.

Taxco

Best place to spend an evening is at **El Jumil,** the disco club up at the Hotel Monte Taxco. Frequently on weekends there is live entertainment at the club, for which a cover is charged. **The Hotel de la Borda** sometimes has nighttime entertainment. In town the top discos are **Tropica** on the plaza (tel. 2–2565), and **Bugambillas** at Juan Ruiz de Alarcon 7 (tel. 2–1836).

Puebla

There is frequently evening entertainment at the hotels **Misión** and **Meson del Angel. Flamingos,** at Teziutlan Norte 1 (tel. 48–0399) features shows at dinner on Friday and Saturday evenings. Discos include **D'Artagnan** at Juarez 2923 (tel. 48–6306), **Porthos** on the Cholula Road (tel. 48–9455) and **Midae** in Cholula (tel. 47–0638).

ACAPULCO
AND IXTAPA/ZIHUATANEJO

Playgrounds Where Fun Reigns

by
SUSAN WAGNER

Susan Wagner is author of Fodor's Fun in Acapulco. *Former travel editor of* Modern Bride *magazine, she has had travel articles published in leading magazines and newspapers throughout the world and has made frequent radio and television appearances on travel programs as an expert on travel to Mexico. She has been studying, visiting, and working in Mexico for many years and claims that she has never had a dull moment during her many visits to Acapulco.*

Acapulco. There's nothing like it in Mexico *or* in the world! Eccentric, mundane, action-packed, tranquil, forthright, beguiling, it's much more than a glittering international playground. It's a multifaceted Mexican city that is among the largest in the country. It's a fun factory that works full shift around the clock around the year. No other resort in the world knows how to manufacture outrageous fun better. Most places that have been blessed with such spectacular scenic beauty and that have added such fabulous facilities for visitors would have stopped right there. But not Acapulco. They take things several steps further and never rest in their efforts to make you have fun every minute of every day of your visit. They make a business of making your vacation unforgettable. That's why Acapulco is so special.

Few places in the world are so permissive. Anything goes, as long as it has nothing to do with breaking the law. This is a place that invites you to let your hair down and kick up your heels, a place where when people say they've danced until dawn, they really mean it! You can stay in your bathing suit past midnight, wear a ball gown to breakfast and no one will bat an eye.

There's so much to see and do that you can plan every day to suit your mood. You can find or make a party from dawn to dusk, or slip away to a secluded spot to revel in unspoiled natural beauty. No matter what you choose, chances are that the temperature will be pleasant and the sun will be shining.

Great weather is Acapulco's ace in the hole. The average year round temperature is 82° F. Generally, the degree of humidity varies more than the temperature throughout the year. Even in the rainy season, August-October, showers are short and most of the rain falls at night. The driest part of the year, December 15 to Easter, is "The Season." Humidity escalates from June to October, but if you don't mind the tropical heat, you can save up to 40% on hotel rates. Generally, everything is open all year round. Christmas and Easter are the most crowded weeks of the year. Book well in advance if you plan to travel during the season.

The weather, the reasonable exchange rates and the amazing attractions are Acapulco's major drawing cards. Of the over one million visitors who arrive annually, many come back every year. Acapulco is not only one of the country's leading resorts for international visitors, it is also the *Numero Uno* destination for Mexican tourists.

Another of Acapulco's greatest assets is that it is thoroughly Mexican. Life goes on as it did centuries ago just off the Costera. The Public Market, Mercado Municipal, is as big as the ones that everyone depends on in other cities, and the downtown area is a bustling tropical port that is also a port of call for cruise ships.

It was the port, not the beaches, that first brought Acapulco world wide attention.

It was popular from the very beginning. The Nahuatl Indians who first lived here called Acapulco "the place where the reeds were destroyed," and indeed it seems that few reeds are left. It was the deep water bay that first brought Acapulco commercial importance. After the Conquest, the Spaniards made it into a leading port for trade with the Orient, and a major take-off point for Spanish colonizers. Hurtado de Mendoza sailed from Acapulco to discover the South Sea Islands and Sebastian Viscaino left from here to discover California. Cortez ordered the settlement of Acapulco in 1531, but it was not until 1799 that Emperor Carlos IV declared it an official city.

A burst of speed in Acapulco's development occurred in the 1950s when an improved highway from Mexico City was completed and the

ACAPULCO

Points of Interest

1) Bull Ring
2) Charro Stadium
3) Cici Children's Marine Park
4) Convention Center
5) Fort San Diego
6) Market
7) Mexican Naval Base
8) Muelle Pier
9) Old Downtown
10) State of Guerrero Tourist Secretariat
11) Tourist Office

Hotels

12) Acapulco Malibu
13) Acapulco Plaza
14) Acapulco Princess
15) Las Brisas
16) Calinda
17) Casa Blanca
18) Condesa Del Mar
19) Copacabana
20) Exelaris Hyatt Continental
21) Exelaris Hyatt Regency
22) La Palapa
23) Pierre Marques and Club de Golf
24) El Presidente
25) Ritz
26) Villa Vera

Shopping Malls

27) Flamboyant
28) Galeria Plaza
29) Paraiso Radisson
30) El Patio
31) Plaza Condesa
32) Plaza Icacos
33) La Vista

crowds began to arrive. From then on, the tropical snowball has been growing at an amazing speed.

There is so much to see and do that you won't be able to fit it all into one visit. Days are spent in the Great Outdoors. Acapulco nights are legendary. Discos that out-glitter any others in the world stay open until the last guest goes home. Some revellers find that another day has begun before they've climbed into bed! That's one of Acapulco's most delicious qualities. Any night will last as long as you can, and the fun never stops until *you* want it to.

EXPLORING ACAPULCO

Acapulco is one of the world's most beautiful bays. Bordered by the golden Pacific on one side and the towering Sierra Madre mountains on the other, it lies in a breathtaking setting 6 hours drive southwest of Mexico City. Flying time is 45 minutes.

The first view of the bay that you get on the ride from the airport will take your breath away. Every time. The Carretera Escenica (Scenic Highway) is a smooth, flat stretch of highway that passes the Princess and Pierre Marques hotels and begins to climb up the hill. Your first panoramic view will be that of tiny Puerto Marques. The next one, just above Las Brisas Hotel, will be glittering Acapulco Bay in all of its glory. The highway then winds around the hillside, passing the world famous Las Brisas Hotel and residential section and La Vista Shopping Mall.

The wide and wonderful Costera Miguel Aleman, one of the world's most exciting seaside highways, begins at the foot of the hill in front of the Naval Base and winds west around the coast as far as Caleta. Just about everything you may want to see or do is on or just off this amazing highway. The portion between the Hyatt Regency and the Radisson Paraiso is called "The Strip." It just may be the most fun-packed stretch of highway anywhere in the world.

Beyond it, the road travels through an underpass and winds on past the cruise ship terminal through the downtown area and out to Caleta, the beach that launched the resort of Acapulco into worldwide stardom. Today, this area is called "Traditional Acapulco." It's a perfect place to enjoy a quiet stay away from the crowds.

Past the downtown area, a road winds up to the famous La Quebrada where the daring divers perform and another goes out to Pie de la Cuesta, a primitive beach that is another super scenic 15-minute ride away. Here, you can watch some of the world's most beautiful sunsets. Coyuca Lagoon, a nature preserve where you can swim and ski in fresh water, is across the street.

Turnoffs from the airport road will take you to Barra Vieja, a rustic village with a few seaside restaurants where you can sun and swim. Beto's-Barra Vieja is best. It also has a pool.

Tres Palos, Acapulco's most primitive lagoon and Costa Chica, an area where African descendants live, can be reached from the Highway 200 turn off. Costa Chica is about 150 miles away.

Wherever you go, whatever you do in Acapulco, chances are that you'll get more than your money's worth. The sunshine and beautiful surroundings are free dividends. This is one of the few places in the world where the fun will last as long as you let it.

PRACTICAL INFORMATION FOR ACAPULCO

HOW TO GET THERE. By Air. Major airlines operating from leading U.S. gateways to Acapulco are: *Aeromexico, American, Continental, Mexicana, Western.* Some companies stop in Mexico City for immigration. Two large bags per person are permitted. There are frequent flights from Mexico City every day. Flying time is about 40 minutes.

By Bus. Two bus lines operate frequent schedules from Mexico City. The trip takes about 7½ hours. Some buses are comfortable and air conditioned. *Estrella de Oro:* Deluxe Service. Tel. 5–95–68; at terminal downtown at Cuauhtemoc and Magallanes. *Flecha Roja;* tel. 2–03–51; Terminal at Cuauhtemoc 97.

By Car. An excellent road, Route 95, links Acapulco with Mexico City. Driving time is approximately 5 hours. Tolls total about $3.50. There is a gas station about every hour. Roadside restaurants are not recommended for gringos. There is an Army Inspection Station 60 kms before Acapulco. The highway is patroled by Green Angels who help out with breakdowns. (See *Facts at Your Fingertips.*) The winding old road takes longer but is free. A detour from the new road to the colonial silver city of Taxco takes about 2½ hours.

PHONES AND EMERGENCY NUMBERS. The area code for Acapulco is 748. To direct dial from Acapulco dial 91 (lada) + area code (clave) + number for domestic calls; 95 + area code + number for international calls to the U.S. and Canada; 98 + area code to the rest of the world. You'll save considerable money if you call home collect (*a cobrar*). There is a hefty 40%-plus telephone tax in Mexico. Hotels usually levy a service charge for every call, regardless of whether the call goes through. It is cheaper to call at night or on weekends, but there seems to be a skeleton crew of operators then. If you want to get through fast, call during the day, and ask your operator how long it will take to get through. Also ask for time and charges when you finish. Dial 02 for operator-assisted calls within Mexico; 09 for international calls.

Public Phones. Mexico is in the process of changing public phones and raising prices. However, a local call in Acapulco still costs 20 centavos or one new peso for three minutes.

Emergency Numbers. *Secretaria de Turismo:* Costera Miguel Aleman, No. 54; tel. 4–61–34 or 4–61–36; *U.S. Consular Representative:* Hotel Club del Sol; tel. 5–66–00. If you speak Spanish, *Police:* tel. 2–00–40; *Traffic Police:* tel. 2–50–34; *Red Cross:* tel. 5–09–43; *Fire Department:* tel. 5–00–73; SEME for medical assistance, tel. 4–32–60.

Airlines. *Aeromexico:* Costera Miguel Aleman 286, or on the second floor above VIP's in the Torre de Acapulco; tel. 5–16–25. *American:* Hotel Condesa del Mar; tel. 4–12–44. *Braniff:* the airport; tel. 4–04–81. *Continental:* the airport, tel. 4–33–08. *Mexicana de Aviacion,* Hotel Las Hamacas or second floor above VIP's in Torre de Acapulco; tel. 4–68–90. *Western:* the airport; tel. 4–07–16.

HOW TO GET AROUND. Getting around in Acapulco is particularly easy. Most of the leading shops, restaurants, hotels and discos are located along the wide Costera and are easy to find. Those staying on The Strip can walk to most major places along it.

From the Airport. This is just about the only transportation set-up in Acapulco that is complicated, haphazard, and uncomfortable. Private taxis are not permitted to carry passengers from the airport to town, a distance of about 14 miles. As many international flights are scheduled to arrive simultaneously, an already complicated system which is definitely not designed for tourists' comfort, and is certainly stacked against those traveling alone, becomes even more unpleasant.

Here's how the system was designed to run; however, it rarely does. Your porter asks the name of your hotel when you leave customs. He drops your bags at that zone. (Signs indicating which zone your hotel is in are posted overhead.) You then have to leave your bags, buy a ticket on a bus, van, or combi and come back to board. Tickets are sold at small white booths. As arriving passengers are generally unfamiliar with the system and are confused, booths are crowded and people push, since there is no room to form lines.

Ask which bus or combi will come first and buy that one. The price difference is slight. Tickets cost about $2.80 per person one way and $4 per person round trip, but prices change frequently. Though ticket vendors push buying round-trip transportation, we recommend buying one way only. You call for return pick-up and often have to spend a lot of valuable sun time waiting for the transportation to arrive. Private taxis are permitted to take you from town *to* the airport. The trip costs approximately $6–$8 and you can leave when you wish.

After buying your ticket, go back to your luggage. (Because of the crowds, porters do not wait.) The planeload of arriving passengers has probably made it impossible for the porter to leave your bags near the zone sign. There will probably be a wait for the bus, and you will have to make sure your luggage gets on it. Sometimes you can get private cars or limos at booth no. 1 outside near the curb that cost anywhere from $12 to $25.

A direct ride to or from the airport takes 20–25 minutes. However, since buses from the airport usually make many stops at a variety of hotels, it may take double that amount of time. The good news is that the Scenic Highway affords spectacular views of the bay and if you are staying on The Strip and make different stops, the trip can help in getting you oriented.

So far, no reliable limousine service is available.

Generally, once you get to your hotel, the nightmare is over and getting around is easy.

By Taxi. Taxis are plentiful, easy to find, and relatively inexpensive. Most taxis are blue and white sedans or VWs. Their top light is *off* when they're free. It is usually cheaper to flag one down in the street than to get one of the fleet from your hotel, as hotel taxis pay for the right to be part of the hotel fleet and pass the cost along to the customers. However, the difference between a hotel taxi and one from the street is only about $.50 to $1 if you are going anywhere downtown to any point on The Strip. Check the price before you enter. Most hotels have average rates posted at the door. Rates are fixed by zones. The average cost for a ride anywhere along The Strip is about $1.–$1.50. At night, rates are slightly higher. Drivers do not expect tips, though Mexicans often leave small change. They often claim not to have change, so come prepared with a few 100-peso coins and 500-peso bills. If you flag a cab down, the price may depend on how much the driver likes your looks, but usually it doesn't exceed what a hotel taxi would charge for the same trip. Often it is half. Some street drivers will ask how much you want to pay. $1.50 is tops for point-to-point ride between the Ritz and the Exelaris Hyatt Regency. If you want to go shopping and/or sightseeing and have your cab wait, make a deal before you get in. The charge is usually $8–$10 per hour. You also can arrange for a guide for sightseeing. The cost is about $60–$70 per day.

By Bus. Public buses run from the zocalo to Caleta—some go direct; others follow the more scenic "Flamingo" route from the zocalo to La Base, the Naval Base, at the end of The Strip. Some go farther out to Puerto Marques. The cost is about 85 pesos from the zócalo to the Exelaris Hyatt Regency, but the trip may not be the most comfortable one you'll ever take. Other buses operate from the Post Office to Puerto Marques and to Pie de la Cuesta. Buses marked *Hornos* take the scenic Costera route. Sheltered stops dot The Strip. Watch your purse or wallet.

By Car Rental. Average daily price for a small, automatic air conditioned car is $65–$75/day including mileage, depending on the size. Jeeps, often called safaris, are about $45/day.

When making reservations, clearly state that you want air conditioning and automatic drive, and reserve in advance if you are visiting Acapulco in season. Note your confirmation number or ask the company for a written one and have it on hand when you pick up the car. Reservations made in the U.S. have a mysterious way of getting lost.

If you plan to rent a car, pick it up at the airport. In this way, you can avoid the arrival hassle. Almost all companies have space at the airport. Here are their downtown addresses: *Budget,* Costera Miguel Aleman, tel. 4–82–00; *Hertz,* Costera Miguel Aleman No. 1945, tel. 5–89–47; *Avis,* Costera Miguel Aleman No. 711, tel. 4–13–42; *Dollar,* Costera Miguel Aleman No. 2148, tel. 4–30–66; *Saad* (jeeps), Costera Miguel Aleman No. 28, tel. 4–34–45; *Sand's,* Costera Miguel Aleman, corner Juan de la Cosa, tel. 4–10–31; *Thrifty,* Costera Miguel Aleman, across from Hyatt Continental Hotel, tel. 4–48–44.

TOURIST INFORMATION SERVICES. *Secretaria de Turismo:* Costera Miguel Aleman No. 54, across from CiCi, tel. 4–61–34. Open from 9 A.M. to 1 P.M. and from 4 P.M. to 7 P.M. They can tell you where to go, what to do and approximately how much it costs. Printed material is almost nonexistent. *SECTUR Coordinacion Regional de Delegaciones de Turismo* is also on the Costera across from Super-Super. They sometimes have maps. Open 8 A.M.–3:30 P.M. weekdays; 10 A.M.–2 P.M. Saturdays; tel. 5–10–41.

ENGLISH LANGUAGE MEDIA. *The News,* a good English-language newspaper with international news, stock prices, comics, etc., is published in Mexico City daily. It usually hits hotel newsstands and beach vendors around 11 A.M. *Sol de Acapulco,* a local English-language newspaper, comes out weekly. You can find it at hotel newsstands. Major U.S. newspapers are sold at some hotel newsstands such as the Acapulco Plaza, the Exelaris Hyatt Regency, etc. If you can't find *The News,* go to Sanborn's or Super-Super. Both also have a good collection of American pocket books and magazines.

TV Cable Channel 72 broadcasts news in English at around 9 A.M. and 8 P.M. daily. Watch cable stations for daily schedules. They aren't written anywhere. If the news doesn't come exactly on schedule, leave the set on and hang in there. At least part of it usually shows up. Some cable programs are also in English, but they are mostly old—and we mean *old*—movies. Get used to missing episodes of your favorite soaps.

American and English films with Spanish subtitles are shown around town. A few of the movie houses are *Cine Salon Rojo* on the zocalo; *Variedades* on

Calle Hurtado de Mendoza near the Municipal Market; *Cinema Flamboyant,* across from the Acapulco Plaza, and *Cinema Costa Azul* at the corner of Colon and Magallanes. All are air-conditioned and serve snacks. You should go in when the film begins because you are usually not allowed to stay through and see it several times, as you might back home. Admission is about 1,000 pesos for the better movie houses. There are usually three shows every night from 4 to 10 P.M.

 TOURS. A variety of tours can be arranged through travel agencies at most hotels. If you can't find what you want, go to the source: *Turismo Caleta* (the largest travel agency in Acapulco), Andrea Doria No. 2, tel. 4–65–70; *American Express,* Costera Miguel Aleman No. 709A, tel. 4–64–13; *Viajes Acuario,* Costera Miguel Aleman, corner Francisco Pizarro, tel. 5–71–00; *Wagon Lits Viajes,* Ave. Costera Miguel Aleman 239, tel. 2–28–61; *Betanzos Tours,* Costera Miguel Aleman No. 98, tel. 4–47–71. Most city tours include main beaches, hotels, residential sections, and shopping areas. Some include the divers at La Quebrada. Arrange through your hotel travel agent. Cost: approximately $15.

Bay Cruises. Several small yachts cruise the bay for a view of the hotel zone and celebrity homes. Cruises leave from downtown docks. The *Hawaiiano* leaves on a sunset cruise at 4:30 P.M. It includes live music and three decks for dancing. Cost: $5.50. The evening cruise leaves at 10:30 P.M. and returns at 2 A.M. It includes dancing to live salsa music and a stop at Roqueta Island for a Hawaiian show. Cost: $6.50. Tel. 2–07–85 for reservations.

The *Bonanza* leaves on 2 ½-hour cruises at 11 A.M. and 4 P.M. from its own dock downtown. Daytime cruises include live music. There is a pool on board. Cost: about $6.00. The *Fiesta Cabaret* cruise sails from the same dock at 7:30 every night except Sunday and includes disco music, a Mexican folklore show, and dinner. Cost: $34. Tel. 2–20–55. Double check all times and prices.

The *Akatiki* cruises the bay twice a day from the Colonial Restaurant dock downtown below San Diego Fort. Daytime cruises leave at 10:30 A.M. and return at 2:30 P.M. and include a stop at Puerto Marques Beach for snorkeling. Price: $31. Includes buffet and open bar. Nighttime cruises leave at 7:30 and return at 10:30. Price: $32. Includes dinner, show, and open bar. Tel. 4–61–40. This is the latest rage. Only the nighttime sail operates on Sundays.

The *Polaris* glass-bottom boat cruise will show you colorful tropical fish and the unique underwater statue of the Virgin of Guadalupe. Stop at Roqueta Island for swimming and a buffet lunch. Price: about $6.

Peregrina, a sailboat, cruises the bay twice a day at 10:30 A.M. and 4:30 P.M. Open bar and bilingual guide. Price: about $12. Tel. 4–14–93.

Safari Tour of exotic Coyuca Lagoon. The ocean is on one side of the road and a freshwater lagoon, which is a nature preserve, is on the other. A haven for nature lovers. Price: $23. Lunch and drinks are included.

The divers at La Quebrada. This is a spectacle that you should see at least once. Dives take place both day and night. Both are dramatic. Divers plunge 30 feet into 1½-meter-deep waters. There is a minimal charge to watch outside on the terraced hillside. You tip the divers afterwards. Or, you can watch from La Perla nightclub at El Mirador Hotel, where the cover charge is $4 per person. Check at your hotel desk or at El Mirador for show times. Many tours include the divers. Nighttime shows are usually at 7:15, 8:15, 9:15, and 10:30.

PARKS AND GARDENS. Papagayo Park is one of the top municipal parks in the country for location, beauty, and variety. It is part of the renovation of Acapulco program which the state undertook a few years ago. Papagayo (named after the hotel that formerly stood on the grounds) occupies 52 acres of prime real estate along the Costera just after the underpass at the end of The Strip. The park offers much more than beautiful paths and walkways. Though it is primarily directed to children, there is plenty for people of all ages to enjoy. For the kids, there is a life-size replica of a galleon like the ones that sailed into Acapulco when it was Mexico's capital for trade with the Orient. There is a race track with mite-sized Can Am cars; a replica of the space shuttle *Columbia;* bumper boats to ride in the lagoon; and other rides. A cable car will carry you from the park to the beach. The Aviary is the park's most spectacular feature. Hundreds of species of birds can be seen as you walk along shaded pathways. Admission to the park is free. There is a charge of 300–1,000 pesos for rides, which operate 2:30–9:30 P.M. on weekdays and 3:30–11:30 P.M. on Saturdays and Sundays, and 100 pesos to the aviary. Rides are closed on Tuesdays.

The Zocalo. The main square in front of the cathedral is pretty and shaded. Free band concerts take place on Sunday afternoon around 6 P.M.

Roqueta Island. The boardwalk that circles Roqueta does not pass as either a park or a garden, but it is one of the most scenic walks to be taken in Acapulco. The tranquility, the untamed foliage, and the spectacular views give you a Robinson Crusoe feeling. Take sneakers. The bridge between the ferry terminal and Palao Restaurant needs repair.

CiCi (Centro Internacional para Convivencia Infantil) is a water-oriented amusement park for children with daily dolphin and seal shows, a swimming pool with waves, a toboggan ride, and other activities. It is open from 10 A.M. to 6 P.M. every day. Admission is 2,000 pesos for adults, 1,500 for children ages 2–10. There is an extra charge for the toboggan ride.

PARTICIPANT SPORTS. Acapulco is a sportsman's paradise. Name your favorite tropical sport and chances are that you'll find it somewhere in town. Water sports prevail and conditions for them are perfect. Your hotel can arrange almost anything. If it can't, or if you can't find it on the beach, here are a few ideas:

Golf. The Princess and the Pierre Marques hotels have two spectacular 18-hole championship courses. Greens fees are about $31 for guests and $41 for all others. Price includes cart. Reservations should be made one day in advance. Call 4–31–00 for the Princess; 4–20–00 for Pierre Marques. There is also a public course of nine holes on the north side of The Strip across from the Elcano Hotel. The greens fee is approximately $8. Call 4–07–81 for reservations.

Deep Sea Fishing. Marlin, sailfish, tuna, snapper, yellowtail mackerel, and bonito are prize catches. Boats that accommodate from four to eight people cost about $100–$150 per day. Food and drink are extra. Excursions usually leave about 7:30 A.M. and return about 2 P.M. You can arrange them for yourself by going to *Pesca Deportiva* downtown on the Costera, just down from Sanborn's on the opposite side of the street. Tel. 2–10–99.

At *Divers de Mexico,* downtown at 100 Costera Miguel Aleman, tel. 2–13–98, you can rent chairs for about $50 or boats from $210–$230. Small boats for freshwater fishing can be rented at *Coyuca Lagoon* across from Pie de la Cuesta, at *Fernando Cadena's,* or *Tres Marias.* You must bring your own tackle. Boats cost about $25 per hour.

Parasailing. This fabulous sport began in Acapulco. A boat will pull your parachute high over the Bay for a thrilling view of it all. A seven-minute ride costs about $5–$7.

Scuba Diving. You can arrange scuba diving excursions at *Divers de Mexico* downtown at 100 Costera Miguel Aleman, tel. 2-13-98, or at *Arnold Brothers* on the Costera in front of San Diego Fort, tel. 2-18-77. At Divers, a four-hour excursion with lessons, equipment and snack costs approximately $50 per person. If you're already a certified diver, the cost is approximately $40; less if you have your own equipment. Arnold Brothers runs three scuba excursions per day for experts as well as beginners. Two-and-one-half-hour trips cost $45.

Snorkeling. It's best to bring your own snorkeling equipment; however, you may be able to rent some on the beach or at one of the restaurants. *Palao Restaurant* near La Roqueta, *Arnold Brothers* or *Divers de Mexico* have some for rent. The cost is minimal.

Tennis. Most hotels have tennis courts. If yours doesn't, chances are you can play at another hotel. It is generally better to bring your own racquet as most clubs do not have rentals. Court fees range from $6.00 to $10.00 per hour, a bit more for night play. Ball boys get 1,000 pesos per hour. Early morning and late afternoon are the most comfortable times to play because of the midday heat. Reserve in advance. Here is a brief rundown on a few of the courts: *Acapulco Plaza:* Costera Miguel Aleman across from Flamboyant Shopping Center; five clay courts lit for night play; tel. 5-80-50. *Acapulco Princess:* 9 outdoor, 2 indoor courts lit for night play, tel. 4-31-00. *Club de Tenis Alfredo's:* Avenida del Prado 29; two outdoor lighted flexipave courts; tel. 4-00-04. *Club de Tenis and Golf:* Costera Miguel Aleman, across from Hotel Malibu; four lighted clay courts; tel. 4-07-81. *Exelaris Hyatt Continental:* Costera Miguel Aleman; two lighted indoor courts; tel. 4-09-09. *Exelaris Hyatt Regency:* Costera Miguel Aleman; five outdoor lighted courts; tel. 4-12-25. *Pierre Marques:* five courts; tel. 4-20-00. *Tiffany's Racquet Club:* Avenida Villa Vera 120; five outdoor clay courts; tel. 4-79-49. *Villa Vera:* Lomas del Mar; three outdoor lighted clay courts; tel. 4-03-33.

Water Skiing. Water skiing was invented in Acapulco. Renting a ski boat from the beach costs about $15–$25 per hour. If two people ski simultaneously, it costs the same. You can take lessons at Club Colonial on the Costera across from San Diego Fort; tel. 3-70-77. They also have a fabulous water ski show.

Windsurfing. Windsurfers are available at *Boca Chica Hotel,* in *traditional Acapulco,* and on Condesa Beach. You can rent hobby cats, broncos, jet skis, and even inner tubes along Condesa Beach. Rates range from $10 to $20 per hour. Giant inner tubes go for a few cents. Kayaks and pedal boats can be rented for pennies on Caleta Beach.

 SPECTATOR SPORTS. Bullfights take place every Sunday afternoon at 5 P.M. at Plaza Caletilla in the old part of town. The best matadors appear in The Season, December to Easter. The best seats are at the railing (barrera) in the shade (sombra). Top price for a ticket is about $10. Your hotel or a local travel agency can arrange an excursion which includes the ticket and transportation to and from the bullring. You can buy a ticket at Motel Kennedy behind Botas Moy; tel. 5-85-40. The office is open daily, 10 A.M.–2 P.M. and 4–7 P.M., Wednesdays through Saturdays, and from 10 A.M.–3 P.M. Sundays.

BEACHES. Acapulco has some of the world's most spectacular beaches. Water temperatures are comfortable and just right for bathing all year round. You can find every kind—crowded or secluded, rough or calm, even fresh or salt water. Most of the popular beaches have names, but few tourists are aware of them and you seldom hear anyone using them. Itinerant vendors sell snacks and souvenirs and restaurants serve light meals under palapas everywhere. Generally, you'll be able to find a secluded place to yourself. There's plenty of room to go around. Wear sandals if you plan to walk any distance. The beach is broad and the sand can get hot! Here is a brief rundown from east to west:

Revolcadero Beach extends beyond the Princess and Puerto Marques hotels. It is wide and sprawling. The water is shallow and waves are fairly rough. Serious swimmers will probably want to swim in the pool.

Puerto Marques is a quiet, hidden bay just off the highway. Conditions are ideal for swimming and water sports. Mexican tourists prevail, and Saturdays and Sundays are crowded. The rest of the week is heaven. Rustic restaurants border the beach. You can rent a chair or a hammock and order up a serenade from strolling musicians. Inner tubes, sun fish and water ski boats can be rented.

Icacos Beach stretches from the Naval Base to El Presidente Hotel. It is broad and sloping. Waves are gentle until late afternoon.

Condesa Beach is the most action packed of all. It lies between the Condesa del Mar and the Ritz hotels. Broad and sloping, it is alive with restaurants, vendors, and people every day. Waves are gentle until late afternoon. There is plenty of shade. You can rent everything from an inner tube to a bronco.

Hornos and Hornitos beaches run from the Condesa del Mar to San Diego Fort. Mexican tourists prevail here. They know a good thing when they see one! These beaches are shaded by graceful palms. Swimming conditions are good. Restaurants are within easy walking distance.

Caleta and Caletilla beaches were once the center of Acapulco's action. The sun is strongest in the morning. Conditions are ideal for swimming. These beaches are frequented by Mexican tourists and locals and are least crowded on weekdays. A day in the sun here is fun. You'll get a taste of what Acapulco was like in days gone by. Ferry boats leave for Roqueta Island and Palao Restaurant. Some boats have glass bottoms and will take you to see the underwater statue of the Virgin de Guadalupe for a few pesos more.

Roqueta Island. A round-trip ferryboat ride costs about $1.50 and takes about 10 minutes. This is another favorite of Mexican tourists which is a wonderful getaway spot on weekdays. Swimming conditions are excellent. Palao Restaurant, a short but sometimes difficult walk away, is good. They have their own mini beach where you can take a dip between courses and rent snorkel equipment. There is a spicy Cuban extravaganza at night with dinner and dancing. Price: about $35 per person.

Pie De La Cuesta, about 15 minutes out of town where Acapulco's first international airport was located, has remained relatively unpopulated. A few rustic restaurants and hotels border the wide and wonderful beach. Palapas provide shade. You can rent a chair or a hammock and have a drink. Horses can be rented to ride along the beach. Waves are high. Nothing more than dip at the water's edge is advisable. Ukae Kim Hotel is a little jewel, where nonguests can use the pool area overlooking the beach for 1,500 pesos a day. Those who want to spend a day swimming or fishing in fresh water or waterskiing on a smooth surface can cross the street to Fernando Cadena's or the popular Tres Marias' rustic "beach clubs" on La Coyuca Lagoon. Tres Marias has good boats for waterskiing and excursions, broncos, and bumper boats.

There are lounges for sunning, and the food is good. Get there early on Sundays if you want a boat. Parts of *Rambo* were filmed in this beautiful, primitive area.

MUSEUMS AND GALLERIES. San Diego Fort has opened as a museum. Pre-Columbian relics found in the area and other historic items relating to the history of the State of Guerrero are on display. The way that the exhibits are arranged is as interesting as the exhibits themselves. This is worth a look. Allow at least ½ hour. Entry fee is 180 pesos (500–1,800 pesos for special exhibits). Open 10 A.M.–6 P.M. Tuesdays–Sundays; closed Mondays. Sundays are gratis. An increasing number of galleries are appearing on the scene. Reasonable exchange rates make paintings and sculptures exceptionally good buys. Here are a few of the galleries from east to west.

Intergalerias in the Princess Shopping Mall features works of Sergio Bustamante. Hours are 10 A.M.–1 P.M. and 4–7 P.M. except Sundays.

Pal Kepenes, fabulously original jewelry, sculptures, and other works by this famous and talented local sculptor are on display for sale in his house near Los Rancheros Restaurant on Guitarron No. 140. Call 4–37–38 for a viewing appointment.

Galeria 2010 (Esteban), Costera Miguel Aleman No. 2010, a short walk East of the Malibu Hotel. This is an amazing combination boutique and art gallery. The gallery displays works of contemporary artists in dramatic architectural surrounding. (See *Shopping* section below.)

Sergio Bustamante, Costera Miguel Aleman 711–B, across from El Tucan boutique. Two floors of whimsical wood, metal, ceramic, and papier-mâché sculptures by Sergio Bustamante. Open 9–9 daily; Sundays, 10 A.M.–2 P.M. El Dorado Gallery, Costera Miguel Aleman 709–D, features the colorful work of Mario Gonzalez, a pupil of Bustamante. Open 9–9 daily; Sundays, 10 A.M.–2 P.M. and 4–8 P.M.

Galeria Victor, El Patio Shopping Center, across from the Hyatt Continental, displays sculptures by popular local artist Victor Salmones whose work is world renowned. Hours: 9:30 A.M.–1 P.M. and 4–8 P.M. except Sundays.

Galeria Rudic, across from the Hyatt Continental Hotel on Costera Miguel Aleman. It features works of world renowned Mexican painters and sculptors, such as Zuniga, Leonardo Nierman, Norma Goldberg, and Jose Luis Cuevas for serious collectors. Hours: 10 A.M.–2 P.M. and 5–8 P.M. It is open on Sundays 10 A.M.–2 P.M.

STAGE, MUSIC, AND DANCE. Cultural programs—symphonies, ballets, etc.—are presented in the Acapulco Centro from time to time. Watch for signs announcing special performances.

SHOPPING in Acapulco has definitely reached sports status. It is easier, better, and more comfortable than ever before. A wider variety of better quality merchandise is available. A few store owners even have the smarts to carry what would be top-of-the-line merchandise anywhere in the world, and a few offer a bit of fall and winter clothing in addition to the plethora of tropical gear. Don't overlook a place that looks old and dusty. That may be the one where you find an unusual bargain. Generally, store hours are from 10 A.M.–1 P.M. and from 4 P.M. to 7 or 8 P.M. Many places are closed on Sundays.

Most visitors alternate doses of shopping with doses of sunning. You can shop in typical markets, tiny boutiques, or glittering malls. Many stores have branches scattered throughout town. Most stores are located just a few steps away from the beach, on the Costera or just off it. Open-air souvenir stalls dot sidewalks. Itinerant vendors bring the market to you, but often prices are not lower than the shops. Look for the 9.25 sterling stamp if you're buying silver. Handicrafts and resort wear are present in profusion and are the most popular buys. Leather goods, jewelry, and decorative items for the home run a close second.

Markets give you a chance to engage in the popular sport of bargaining, which is part of the fun. The *Mercado Municipal* is for those who want to take in a lot of local color as they buy. This sprawling market is as typical as any in Mexico and an integral part of Acapulco life. Like any authentic Mexican market, you'll find anything from pets to peanuts and more. The market spreads over several city blocks and, even though it may not appear so, it is arranged in sections. If you are looking for something particular, learn the name of what you want to buy in Spanish and ask peole to direct you when you get there. With patience and pointing, chances are you'll find it. If you're just going to browse and/or buy souvenirs, enter through the flower section at the corner of Ruiz Cortines and Hurtado de Mendoza streets. You'll find handicrafts to your right and left, inside and outside. Just before Christmas is a wonderful season to be there. Mexican Christmas ornaments are whimsical, amusing, and cost far less than they do back home.

The *Mercado de Artesanias* downtown offers handicrafts, dresses, serapes, and other typical souvenirs. Although this is strictly for tourists, it has the air of an authentic Mexican market as well. In the ceramics section you can order a lamp base, a plate, or a decorative item and watch a talented artisan paint a design to match your color scheme back home. Don't rely on their packing. It's bad. Small stores on the street at the back of the market on Vasquez de Leon and the old-fashioned souvenir shops downtown on the Costera just past the zócalo where locals buy are also fun to browse.

Noa Noa is a smaller handicrafts market on the corner of the Costers and Hurtado de Mendoza, at the turnoff for the Mercado Municipal. It has the same merchandise that you'll find downtown, but less local color.

AFA, Artesanias Finas, is a handicrafts supermarket on the corner of Horacio Nelson and James Cook Avenues. This is an air conditioned place where you can buy souvenirs from throughout the country with credit cards. Though quantity sometimes makes up for quality, and prices are slightly higher than you might find elsewhere, this is probably the easiest place to purchase souvenirs or gifts for the folks back home. Their packing and shipping is about the best.

Resort wear and decorative items are for sale throughout town. The greatest profusion of shops and boutiques lies on both sides along the Costera, between the Malibu and the Acapulco Plaza hotels. Most hotels have a few good stores and boutiques. However, if you seek comfort, large fitting rooms and service, you might prefer to shop in one of the malls. If your size is not available, some stores will make up items in a day or two.

Shopping Malls. Mexicans call a shopping mall *"Centro Comercial."* There are several good ones for those who like to do all their shopping in one place. Here are a few of the best listed from East to West:

The Princess. For those who like to shop in controlled environment, air-conditioned places, the Princess has a collection of about 25 shops, which sell everything from souvenirs to jewelry. *Marietta's* and *Pitti Palace* are two of the finest clothing stores. *Emil's* and *Ricardo's* offer good, medium-priced sportswear. *Emi Fors, Ronay,* and *Bulgary* (no relation to the Italian firm) offer good jewelry. *Intergalerieas* features the work of Sergio Bustamante, a renowned Mexican artist and sculptor.

La Vista, across from Las Brisas Hotel, is one of the most upscale malls in town. It looks like a Mediterranean village overlooking the bay. This is the most comfortable place to shop in Acapulco. Fitting rooms are more spacious and service is more personal and of better quality than what you find along the Costera. *Ore, Marietta, Girasol, Benny's,* and *Antheus* for resort wear; *Oceano Pacifico* for sportswear; *Gucci* and *Aries* for leather goods; and *Tane* for silver are a few of the stores.

Plaza Icacos is a new minimall next to the naval base with a good furniture store, *Lorea,* and a few boutiques.

The *Centro Acapulco* (the Convention Center) has a handful of stores that are open weekdays from 9 A.M. to 5 P.M.

There are two arcades under *Carlos 'n Charlie's. Sergio's Istar,* one of the top boutiques in town, is at the back of *Fingers Arcade,* on the left.

Plaza Condesa, a new multilevel shopping mall, which is one of the largest in town, is across from Condesa del Mar Hotel. It has good clothing and jewelry shops and El Trapiche, a nice snack bar. The Flying Indians of Papantla perform here.

El Patio, farther down the Costera, was one of the first shopping malls on the scene and is still one of the best. The branches of *Marietta's* and *Thelma's*—where local ladies have their clothes made—are here, along with *Gucci* and *Galeria Victor,* one of the prettiest art galleries in town.

El Flamboyant, across from the Acapulco Plaza, has a good collection of stores and boutiques. *Mar y Mar* offers especially colorful resort wear.

The *Acapulco Plaza Hotel* has a spectacular new two-floor shopping gallery with over 48 stores and boutiques. *Diva, Pasarela* (which has world-class beaded dresses), and *Banana Republic* are among the top places. *Tane* and *Pineda de Taxco,* two of the best silver shops, are also here. *Emi Fors* is across the entranceway. *Casual Aca* and *Pitti Palace,* inside near the newsstand, are also good.

Most of the popular separate boutiques lie between the Malibu Hotel and the Diana traffic circle. This area is jam packed with them.

Esteban's *Galeria 2010* is a new concept. It combines a top boutique with a serious art gallery. Esteban is one of the few Mexican designers who export to the U.S. He is famous for both resort wear and evening clothes. The boutique has a "Grand Finale" year-round salesroom and a knockout collection of original costume jewelry. The art gallery is next door.

Acapulco Joe, across from El Presidente Hotel, is king of them all and has gained the coveted status of "Numero Uno," the same position that Carlos n' Charlie's holds on the restaurant scene. *Ralph Lauren Polo* (Mexican made) runs a close second.

Marietta's, Emil's, Benny's, Maraca, and *Mando's* are a few of the other favorites. *Fiorucci, Guess,* and *Express* have brought a new trendy look to the scene. *Favian* and *Anna's* are good "high fashion" places. These are just a few. You're sure to discover a personal favorite.

Samy's, downtown on Calle Hildalgo No. 7, is a wonderful hole-in-the-wall where many celebrities shop. Men's and women's resort wear—made to order and off the rack—are sold at reasonable prices. Talking with Samy, whose real name is Armando, is a treat. By popular demand, Samy may open an "uptown" branch at 21A Rocasola, behind Pizza Hut. Call 2–16–18 to find out.

Don't overlook the bathing suits. Some are terrific and cost far less than they would back home. Mexican tennis clothes are also good and well priced. *Head, Ellesse,* and *Fila* franchises are here in profusion.

Marti, a glittering multilevel sporting goods store at the Diana traffic circle beside soon-to-open Marbella Mall, has everything you need to practice almost any sport.

Here are a few other exceptionally good places:

Leather. *Gucci,* across from El Presidente Hotel, is a Mexican franchise. Some items are undetectable from the genuine ones. *Aries,* in La Vista, is also good.

Silver. *Pineda de Taxco, Tane,* and *Emi Fors,* in the Acapulco Plaza, are among the best. *Taxco el Viejo,* in old Acapulco, has a big collection of traditional silver items.

Sundries. Major stores for sundries, cosmetics and toiletries are: *Sanborn's* on The Strip next to Condesa del Mar, *Woolworth's* downtown; the huge brand new *Gigante* and *Super Super,* the big supermarkets just after the Costera underpass. Sanborn's and Super Super are open all day long 8 A.M.–10 P.M. every day, weekends included. Woolworth's is open every day 9:30. A.M.–8:30 P.M. Gigante keeps similar hours.

Farmacias (drugstores) are everywhere, but many are closed on Sundays. If you need an over-the-counter medicine, try *Sanborn's* first.

RESTAURANTS. Acapulco restaurants are legendary. You can dine up on the hill with a view on down by the sea under a thatched roof palapa. You can have fast food or ethnic food, Mexican or American. You can opt for formal (although gentlemen never need ties or jackets), air conditioned gourmet restaurants, or informal open air seaside places where all you need is a bathing suit and a cover up. Choices are endless. All you have to do is select to suit your mood. Fresh seafood and meat head most menus. Mexican specialties like ceviche (marinated fish), enchiladas (rolled baked tortillas with chicken, cheese or meat inside) or tacos are also popular. Generally, service is good. Acapulco waiters have a special tongue-in-cheek humor and will usually be delighted to join your conversation if you let them.

Average cost for a lunch or dinner in a medium-priced restaurant is $15–$20 with beer or domestic wine. You can still dine in tiny sidewalk places like Pepe's, Las Tablitas and El Rodeo for under $12 for two. Ordering anything imported such as caviar, herring, etc., will push the price way up. Major credit cards except Diners Club and Carte Blanche are accepted in most places except the very small ones. There is at 15% VAT (Value Added Tax) on food and beverages. Most international visitors lunch by the sea and move across the Costera or up the hill for dinner.

If you want to get double your money's worth and have great people watching along with your meal, switch to Mexican hours. Lunch, generally the main meal of the day, is between 2 and 5 P.M. Dinner is between 9 and 11 P.M. Call ahead for dinner reservations in season between December 15 and Easter.

Leisurely dining in a beautiful sunny setting or with a starry view of the Bay is what Acapulco is all about.

Chinese

Shangri La. Calle Picuda No. 5, just off the Costera. Open 6 P.M. to 1 A.M. tel. 4–13–00. Cantonese specialties in a shaded, open air garden. Moderate prices.

Japanese

Suntory, Costera Miguel Aleman across from El Embarcadero. Open P.M.–1 A.M.; tel. 4–80–88. Authentic Japanese cuisine and garden. Meals are served Benihana style.

German

Terraza las Flores. Downtown on the west side of the zócalo; tel. 3–94–63. No nonsense; good, hearty servings of German specialties on a balcony overlooking the plaza. Open 11 A.M.–1 A.M.

Italian

Villa Demos. Avenida del Prado No. 6. Open 7 P.M.–midnight; tel. 4–20–40. A tried and true family trattoria that is a favorite with locals and visitors. Dine under the trees in a pretty wooded garden. European atmosphere and good cuisine.

Spaghetti House. El Patio Shopping Center. Open 5 P.M.–1 A.M.; tel. 4–17–88. An informal hideaway; brick oven pizza and other Italian specialties.

Da Raffaello. Avenida Costera Aleman 1221, second floor across from Condesa del Mar. Open 2 P.M.–1 A.M.; tel. 4–01–00. Good Italian specialties overlooking the Costera.

Dino's. Costera Miguel Aleman 137 across from Crazy Lobster; tel. 4–00–37. An old favorite for dishes with plenty of northern Italian flavor; inside or under the stars; lunch and dinner.

Spanish

El Parador La Vista. Carretera Escenica, La Vista Shopping Center. Open 12:30 P.M.–12:30 A.M.; tel. 4–80–20. Best view of the bay, bar none. The typical appetizers "tapas" are tops.

Sirocco. Costera Miguel Aleman across from Super Super. Open from 1 P.M.–midnight; tel. 2–32–30. Acapulco tradition with authentic Spanish flavor. Paella is the specialty.

Mexican

Los Arcos, Acapulco Plaza Hotel. Air-conditioned. Mexican food with excellent explanations on the menu. Open 6:30 P.M.–12:30 A.M. daily. Live music sometimes. Tel. 5–80–50.

Los Rancheros. Carretera Escenica below Las Brisas Hotel. Open 12:30 P.M.–12:30 A.M.; tel. 4–19–08. A million-dollar view combined with reasonably priced favorite Mexican dishes. Go for the view, not for the food.

La Margarita. Avenida Anahuac No. 110. Brand new; open 6 P.M.–midnight; tel. 4–43–50. The kind of Mexican food that you've come to know and love back home served in a beautiful colonial setting.

Pancho's. Costera Miguel Aleman, near Disco Beach. Open from 1 P.M.–midnight; tel. 4–43–50. The only Mexican restaurant just a few steps from the ocean. You can watch the kitchen prepare your favorite dish.

Gourmet

Note: These are all top dollar restaurants. Meals run up to $40 per person, without wine.

Le Gourmet. Princess Hotel. Fine food in plush airconditioned comfort. This is for big spenders who like to dine in refined surroundings. Soft piano music; continental and French dishes à la carte; beautiful presentation. Snails, sea bass, soups, and desserts are superb. Tel. 4–31–00. Open 7 P.M.–midnight daily.

Miramar. A beautiful new open-air restaurant in La Vista, overlooking the bay. Grand proportions and style with the look of a private home. Start with a drink at the bar to appreciate the amazing architecture and the view. A waterfall cascades at one side of the elegant dining room. Continental cuisine prepared by international chefs. Part of Mexico City's prestigious del Lago chain. Open 6:30 P.M.–12:30 A.M. tel. 4–48–75. Closed Sundays.

Maximillian's in the Acapulco Plaza Hotel is the only air-conditioned gourmet restaurant on the beach. Soft blue decor, comfortable plush banquettes, soft piano music. Continental cuisine presented with European flair à la carte. Desserts are especially delicious. Open 7 P.M.–midnight daily; Tel. 5–80–50.

Normandie. This long-time favorite on the scene is said to be one of the best French restaurants in the country. It has tropical old world charm. The menu comprises what is fresh in the market. Open from June-November only, 6 P.M.–midnight. Costera on the corner of Malaespina Street beside Sol de Acapulco. Dinner $15–$20; tel. 5–19–16 or 5–13–35.

Coyuca 22 has a formal feeling although it is open air. It's a quiet world apart on top of a hill in Old Acapulco, with a view of the other side of the bay. This is not the place to go if you are in a loud party mood. Simple food; high prices. Open daily from December 1 to April 30, 7:00 P.M.–12:30 A.M.; tel. 2–34–68.

Regina. Plaza Icacos beside Exelaris Hyatt Regency; tel. 4–86–53. A new, refined place where waiters wear black ties and soft music plays in the background. Continental cuisine yet to be proved. Dinner only.

Popular Places

Most of these places have a view of the Costera but that doesn't spoil the fun. They are favorites with locals as well as visitors.

El Campanario. High on the hill overlooking everything. Pretty, giant restaurant with the atmosphere of an elegant Italian villa. Mediocre Continental cuisine and slow service, but the views are spectacular. Comfortable bar. Tel. 4–88–30.

Cocula. Next to Bancomer, tel. 4–50–79. One of the best. Try to get a table downstairs under the trees. There is an air-conditioned hideaway bar. Open 7 P.M.–1:30 A.M.

El Embarcadero. It looks like a Polynesian jungle, across from Suntory, complete with thick foliage and screaming monkeys. You sit in a shaded open air "Warehouse." The menu is Oriental too. Malaysian shrimp, chicken Rangoon, Bangkok filet tidbits, etc. Open 6 P.M.–midnight; tel. 4–87–87.

D'Joint. Near the cylindrical Calinda Acapulco, this old favorite specializes in roast beef and rib-eye steaks in steakhouse setting upstairs. Downstairs is strictly for hamburgers, sandwiches, and cable TV. Open nightly from 7 P.M. to 1 A.M.; tel. 4–37–09.

Hard Times. Steaks, ribs, and tacos along with lobster and shrimp are served up on the second floor across from the Calinda. You can enjoy them in an air-conditioned dining room or outside under a palm tree that grows through the floor. Open daily 6:30 P.M.–12:30 A.M.; closed Wednesdays; tel. 4–00–64. The sign is hard to find. Look for red neon lights over the street entrance awning.

Chez Guillaume. Just off the Costera across from the Torre de Acapulco at 110 Avenida del Prado. Continental cuisine with French flair under the stars, overlooking the Costera. Air-conditioned bar. Open Mon.–Sat. from 6:30 P.M. to 12:30 A.M.; tel. 4–12–31 or 4–12–32.

Kycho's. Across from the side of Baby O; tel. 4–07–05. Popular and fun. You can sometimes get smoked salmon here. Crazy games of "Loteria" (Mexican bingo) and backgammon tournaments are played Wednesday nights, but you can hustle up a backgammon game almost any night. Open 2 P.M.–2 A.M. every day but Sunday.

Madeiras. Romantic, ultra chic "Town and Country" decor with a breathtaking view near Las Brisas. Reservations are hard to get. Call at least two days in advance in season and be on time! Allow time for a drink at the pretty bar before you go to the table. Tiny croissants and beautiful table settings by famous Taxco silversmiths, Los Castillo. Dinners are prix fixe at $15, without wine. Seatings at 7 and 9 P.M. Tel. 4–43–78 or 4–69–21.

Papacito's Last Call & Barbecue. Galeria Acapulco Plaza. Fun, tongue-in-cheek ambience. Colonial decor. Lively, live music; air-conditioned. Open late night (7 P.M.–4 A.M.) for light Mexican snacks and ribs.

Pepe & Co. Upstairs above the Costera across from the Condesa del Mar. This is one of the town's top favorites. It has the atmosphere of a private club. You can begin and end the evening in the air-conditioned piano bar and dine outside on the balcony in between. Continental cuisine that tastes as good as home cooking. Everybody seems to know everybody. Open for lunch and dinner 1 P.M.–midnight; closed for lunch on Sundays; tel. 4–70–88 or 4–70–89.

Carlos 'N Charlie's. This popular place packs 'em in every day, except Tuesdays. Everyone who comes to Acapulco seems to pass through these portals at least once. It doesn't open until 6:30 P.M. but the line starts to form around 6. A big air-conditioned bar, crazy waiters, and a flip menu make it fun as well as tasty. You're likely to find the waiter at a disco later. No reservations. You have to wait your turn. Tel. 4–12–85.

Seaside Spots

These are some of the most carefree dining places in the world. You need wear nothing more than a bikini with a cover-up. Chances are that you can samba with your shoes off between courses, or live it up as long as you like—even right through the sunset and into the night. Strolling photographers are there to record the mayhem. Most of the most popular seaside places are between the Condesa del Mar and the Hyatt Continental.

Beto's, under a cool palapa, is one of the old time favorites that everybody has loved since the '50s. It has some delicious dishes that other places don't serve, such as quesadillas de cazon (tortillas filled with baby shark meat and fried) and pescado a la Talla (a split snapper barbecued in a delicious sauce). Live music for dancing if the spirit moves you. Occasional live music. Open daily 10 P.M.–midnight; tel. 4–94–73. No *Diners Club* or *Carte Blanche*.

Beto's Safari Bar has an ultraromantic restaurant hidden away on a downstairs deck overlooking the ocean. Dinner only. Try to get a table by the railing if you're with a loved one.

Barbas Negras (Blackbeard's). High up overlookign the ocean, it serves up hearty food that a pirate might like. A big salad bar and he-man-size helpings of lobster thermidor, shrimp, and steaks. Open daily 6:30 P.M.–midnight; tel. 4–25–49.

Mimi's Chili Saloon. When you're dying for a hamburger, onion rings, potato skins, or French fries, this is your place. Two floors of tasty fast food and a crazy happy hour with twofer mango and strawberry margaritas that will knock your block off. Open daily 6 P.M.–midnight.

Paradise. This has to be the craziest place on the Costera. Absolutely anything goes! Pandemonium prevails just off the beach under the sign of the Red Snapper. Live music keeps the party rolling. Waiters go wild when there's a birthday or anniversary to celebrate. A trained chimpanzee will mug for you and the camera. These and other surprises may interrupt your meal but you'll love it! Shrimp and snapper are the most popular dishes. One of these main courses and you won't have to eat for the rest of the day. Open noon–midnight; tel. 4–59–88.

The Crazy Lobster (Langosta Loca) is not crazy at all. It is serious about its food and it's one of the most dignified of the seaside restaurants. Blonde wood furniture and stucco walls give it a sleek look. Sit on the left if you don't want to be bothered by beach vendors. Pretty, pleasant, good value. Open noon–midnight; tel. 4–59–74.

Mahalo, by the beach or Herman Cortes Street behind the Acapulco Plaza Hotel. New and slightly expensive ($30–$35) but Oriental specialties are served in a pretty setting to the sound of the waves. Dinner only; open 6:30 P.M.; tel. 5–20–51.

Su Casa. It *is* the owner's cozy home. Overlooking the Convention Center and the bay, you get a cosy homey feeling that makes it evident your friendly hosts are present. Simple, easy to order, meat and fish menu. Rose of tomato vinaigrette and conch appetizers are great. Open every night from 6:00 P.M. to midnight; tel. 4–43–50.

Barbarroja (Redbeard). Costera Miguel Aleman across from Fiesta Tortuga. This is really open-end dining under the stars, overlooking the ocean. If pirates had a steakhouse this is what it would look like. Meat, fish, surf and turf plus an air-conditioned piano bar. Open 6:30 P.M.–12:30 A.M. every night. Reserve a table by the sea, the sidewalk is too close for comfort. Tel. 4–59–32.

Sleek and Sexy

Villa Vera Hotel & Racquet Club. A chic restaurant overlooking the Bay, where lunches are lively events and dinners are ultra-romantic. The restaurant has three spectacular views: the bay, the bar and pool area, and the people. Soft piano music at night. Delicious dishes like sole Orly with a curry dip and caramel bananas. Open noon–midnight; tel. 4–03–33.

Sunset Beach Club. A pretty swinging place with international flavor overlooking the ocean, next to Eve disco. Head your raft to the edge of the pool and watch the boys or girls go by on the beach below. Swim-up bar, just the right amount of creative chaos. Open noon–6:30 P.M.; tel. 4–00–92 or 4–34–64.

A new beach club will soon open nearby in the Marbella Mall.

Inexpensive

La Fogata de Charly. A hole-in-the-wall at No. 145 Costera Miguel Aleman, that has a reasonable prix fixe tourist lunch menu that can't be beaten. Prices are low at night, too, and they throw in a free folklore show with cock fights, rope tricks, and dancers. Open noon–midnight.

Pepe's Las Tablitas. On the sidewalk across from Nacional Financiera down from Acapulco Plaza. Specials with chimmichuri and chicken enchiladas with green sauce are tops. Wooden tables, concrete floor; good value served by a Las Brisas graduate; open noon to midnight daily; no reservations.

 NIGHTLIFE. Acapulco is the city in Mexico whose night life is world-renowned. Acapulco nights are as star spangled, dazzling and kinetic as they come. If you *really* adjust to Mexican schedules you can have another full day of fun after dark. When the sun goes down, shimmering lights illuminate the bay and Acapulco begins to dazzle like no other city in the world. Discos that outglitter any others stay open until the last guest goes home. Some revelers find that another day has begun before they've climbed into bed! That's one of Acapulco's most delicious qualities. Any night will last as long as you can, and the fun never stops until *you* want it to. Choices of what to do after dinner are endless. Everything from a moonlight cruise around the Bay to a Mexican Fiesta night is available.

Discos

The outrageous discos are what launched Acapulco nights into international fame. They defy any others to outglitter them. Balloons, confetti, video screens and other surprises add to the pandemonium on the dance floor. In season, they're as dark and as crowded as they come, but that only makes everyone more anxious to get in.

Most have door charges of about $8–$10 per person, more if there is a special show. Domestic drinks cost approximately $2.50–$3.50; imported drinks such as scotch cost $5–$6. A bottle of imported champagne costs $110–$115.

Getting in may not be easy. Often you have to wait outside in a crowd. The best way to get in on a busy night in season is to look classy, sexy, and dignified. Being past your teens helps. Remember that one of the doorman's jobs is to fill the place with the most attractive people he can find. Go around 11 P.M. on a weekend if you want to get in by midnight. However, if you don't feel like waiting, go to *any* disco. They all offer plenty of pandemonium. All are on the Costera unless stated otherwise. All accept major credit cards except *Diner's* and *Carte Blanche*. And most have boutiques, so you can shop between dances!

The Big Eight are: **Baby O, Bocaccio, Cats, Eve, Fantasy, Jackie O, Magic,** and **Midnight Fantasy,** beside La Vista Mall in Las Brisas, is crème de le crème and first class all the way. It has floor-to-ceiling picture windows around a dance floor that overlooks the bay and spectacular laser lights. An inside glass elevator takes you to the "sex shop" on the second floor, which sells lingerie. Entry fee is about $12. Fireworks spilling over the ceiling in the early A.M. make it more than worthwhile. Tel. 4–67–27.

Baby O, across from the Romano Palace, is king of the discos on or near the Strip. Steep stairs with tiers of tables lead to the dance floor, where disco mania prevails. Video screens add to the fun. The crowd outside may be big, but it's worth waiting if you are determined to dance in one of the hottest places in town.

Bocaccio, five minutes down the Strip, is a superfun, time-tested favorite with Acapulco habitués. The momentum never stops. Party gimmicks, balloons, confetti, ethnic hour, video screens, and electronic boards that can personalize welcomes, birthdays, etc., add to the wonderful pandemonium. Tel. 4–19–00.

Cats, behind Midnight, is a pretty, big, new place that everyone seems to like. Comfortable tables, tiered booths, "trees" with sparkling lights, and videos make it even prettier. Tel. 4–73–35.

Eve, formerly UBQ, is just before the traffic circle. It is the only disco on the ocean. The dance floor may suddenly open so you can dance under the stars. There is a comfortable bar and a few video games.

Jackie O is another old favorite that used to be called Charlie's Chili. Mirrors, leaded glass windows, and plush booths make it look like a private club. There is a bar upstairs. Unaccompanied women are admitted. Tel. 4–08–43.

Midnight, which was Le Jardin, is the most modern-looking of them all. The Villa Vera crowd comes here. More than any other, the people are "the show." Few gimmicks distract from the dance floor. Tel. 4–82–95.

Jackie O, Baby O and Magic have snack bars where you can refuel your engine. Remember, an Acapulco disco rule of thumb is: If you can't get into one, go to another.

Gay Discos

Gay discos are an integral part of Acapulco's nighttime scene. Three of them are just off the Costera across from D'Joint on Avenida de los Deportes. **The Gallery** has an opulent show of female impersonators that is popular with everybody. Shows are at 11:30 P.M. and 1:30 A.M., nightly except Sunday; tel. 4–34–97. Cost: $10.00 plus drinks. **Peacock Alley** probably has the best music in town. The bar and dance floor are under white "palm trees." **Disco 9** is the smallest of the three.

Hotel Discos and Nightclubs

Several hotels have lively disco clubs that also feature shows and big name entertainment. **Cocoloco** and **Tiffany's** in the Princess, tel. 4–31–00; **Club Banneret** in the Calinda, two shows daily except Monday at 11:30 P.M. and 1:30

A.M. Tel. 4–04–10; **Mil Luces** in the Exelaris Hyatt Regency, tel. 4–38–88; two shows nightly at 11:30 P.M. and 1:30 A.M., and **Poseidon Disco Show** in Hotel Torres Gemelas are just a few of them. Check to find out show times. **El Fuerte,** in front of Las Hamacas Hotel, has a fabulous flamenco show twice a night except Sunday. **Nina's Tropical Disco** is for those who like it Latin and lively.

Rooftop Supper Clubs

Several rooftop supper clubs offer traditional dining and dancing overlooking the bay. The atmosphere is quieter and more romantic. Most feature continental cuisine and live music for touch dancing. Dress codes are slightly more formal (no blue jeans, please), but gentlemen still never need socks, ties, or jackets.

La Joya in the Exelaris Hyatt Continental, tel. 4–09–09; **Numero Uno** in the Exelaris Hyatt Regency, tel. 4–28–88; **Techo Del Mar** in the Condesa del Mar, tel. 4–23–55; and **La Fragata** in the Acapulco Paraiso Hotel are the best. La Joya and Numero Uno sometimes close after the season, so call to check.

Raunchy but Fun

Chippendale's, a male strip joint, just opened on the site of the old Estacion Acapulco. It incorporates an antique train car! **Tipsy's Bar** is beside it. **La Huerta,** in the red light district, is fun if you don't flirt with another man's girl. **Quinta Rebecca** is for those who are interested in more than dancing.

Happy Hours

Almost every hotel has a happy hour, especially during the season. Most take place 6–8 P.M. and offer live music for dancing and twofer drinks. The Acapulco Plaza (where you pay by the drink), El Presidente and Condesa del Mar are among the best. This is a time to meet and greet if you're in the mood.

FOR THE KIDS. Big hotels like the Hyatt and the Acapulco Plaza stage special activities for children. Most take place around the pool. Watch for the daily bulletin under your door. **Miniature golf** can be played in front of Super Super at Golfito. There is a **Go Kart** and **roller skating** rink behind Big Boy. It also has electronic games. Downtown, **Chispas** just off the zocalo on Calle Hidalgo also has electronic games. Latin discos **Le Dome** and **Magic,** across from the Acapulco Plaza, sometimes have *tardeadas* for teenagers on Sunday afternoons. No alcoholic beverages are served, but the same party pandemonium as every night prevails. Entry fee is usually about $1.

HOTELS. Acapulco's amazing accommodations range from a *De Luxe* category to trailer parks. Almost all of them have more spacious rooms, more beautifully gardened pools, and larger public areas than their counterparts in other parts of the world. And most of them are no more than a few minutes' walk away from a beautiful beach. Almost all have pools, several restaurants, and live music in the bar. Which one you choose and the location play a big part in determining your vacation lifestyle. For those who like to have everything top-of-the-line and on-the-premises, the slightly isolated Princess and Pierre Marques and Las Brisas hotels will fill the bill. Hotels on The Strip from the Exelaris Hyatt Regency to the Acapulco Paraiso are right in the middle of the action. Generally rates go down as you get nearer town. Beyond it is Traditional Acapulco, where some of the hotels that were Acapulco's first drawing cards still stand. These tend to be smaller, quieter, and more relaxing than bigger properties. Most are a short walk from the beach and have small pools. Those that do not have air conditioning have overhead fans.

The season when the weather is best and the rates are highest, is December 15–Easter. If you are planning to go for Christmas, Washington's Birthday, or Easter, book as far ahead as you can to avoid disappointment. Rates go down as much as 40% after that. Especially reasonably priced packages usually become available between July and September. Watch your local newspaper for special offers.

The following is a sample of what is available. Hotels are listed below by the average peak-season rate, in the following categories, based on double occupancy: *Deluxe,* $150 and up; *First class,* $100 to $150; *Expensive,* $50 to $100; *Moderate,* $20 to $50; *Inexpensive,* $20 and below. Rates quoted are subject to change without notice and are European plan (EP) with no meals, unless otherwise stated.

Deluxe

Acapulco Princess, Playa Revolcadero, Apartado Postal No. 1351. 1031 rooms; tel. 4–31–00. Grand style, self contained, 8 minutes from the airport; ½ hour from The Strip. This is for those who like to have everything, but *everything* on the premises—all 380 acres of it! Tennis, golf, nightclub, disco, restaurants. Spectacular pool area with salt and fresh water pools, beautiful gardens. Golf and tennis.

Las Brisas. Box 281, Carretera Escenica 5255; tel. 4–16–50; U.S. reservations (800) 228–3000. 300 Casitas, all with private or shared pool, on the hill overlooking the bay. Pink and white staff-driven jeeps take you from reception to your room and to the beach club below. Tennis courts, restaurants, and health clubs. Elegant and exclusive with the air of a private club. This is the only hotel whose facilities are *not* open to the public. Your neighbor is likely to be a celebrity or an astronaut. No children.

Pierre Marques. Playa Revolcadero (beside the Princess) Apartado Postal 474; tel. 4–20–00. 340 rooms and duplex villas. Restaurants, golf, tennis, three fresh water pools. All facilities are interchangeable with Acapulco Princess. Shuttle bus between the properties takes 10 minutes. Quieter, sprawling property, beautiful gardens and villas, tranquil setting.

Villa Vera Hotel & Racquet Club. Box 260 Lomas del Mar No. 35; tel. 4–03–33; U.S. reservations: (800) 233–4895. The prettiest small hotel on the Strip, with 79 photogenic rooms and suites, all different, some with private pools. Cable TV, beautiful gardens, a popular bar, and a pool area with the country's first swim-up bar. One of the town's most popular restaurants overlooks the bay. Tennis courts, plush private-club atmosphere. Facilities are interchangeable with Maralisa Hotel on the beach, a 5–7 minute ride away, but guests seldom leave the pool. Management discourages children.

First Class

Acapulco Plaza. Box C-88, Costera Miguel Aleman No. 22; tel. 5–80–50, U.S. (800) 238–8000. 1000 rooms and suites. Full service self-contained resort on The Strip. Tennis, pools, health club, restaurants, cable TV, sparkling new shopping mall. Everything you need for fabulous fun in the sun is here. Plenty of action just outside. Five sensational restaurants. Lively happy hour. Oasis Health Club (no children). Four tennis courts.

Exelaris Hyatt Regency. Box 565 Costera Miguel Aleman No. 1; tel. (800) 228–9000. 694 rooms at the foot of the scenic highway at the beginning of The Strip. Tennis courts, restaurants, night clubs. Almost all rooms view the Bay. Elegant atmosphere. A short walk away from "the action."

Expensive

Acapulco Ritz. Costera Miguel Aleman just before underpass; tel. 5–73–36; U.S. (800) 458–6888; 278 rooms. Newly remodeled; attractive new seaside dining room. Families like this one.

Acapulco Tortuga. Costera Miguel Aleman; tel. 4–88–89, U.S. (800) 223–2633; 250 rooms. Across the street from the beach in the middle of the action.

Calinda/Acapulco. Costera Miguel Aleman No. 1260; tel. 4–04–10; 366 rooms with balconies. Cylindrical, beach side, newly refurbished.

Condesa Del Mar. Box 933 Costera Miguel Aleman No. 1220; tel. 4–28–81, U.S. (800) 228–3728. Restaurants, pools, tennis, rooftop night club right in the "action" a few steps away from your front door. Never-a-dull-moment atmosphere. Happy Hour pandemonium in the lobby is a sight to see.

Las Hamacas. Costera Miguel Aleman on the curve before town; Box 399; tel. 2–61–66. A pretty, updated old favorite with a small palm-shaded pool. Across the street from the beach.

Hotel do Brazil. Costera Miguel Aleman 252, across from Hornitos Beach; tel. 5–07–74. 120 rooms. Brazilian flavor. TV, service, bar, pool; Brazilian extravaganza every night except Sundays.

Hyatt Continental. Box 214, Costera Aleman; tel. 4–09–09, U.S. (800) 228–9000. 435 rooms on eight floors. Restaurants, rooftop night club, pool. Facilities interchangeable with Exelaris Hyatt Regency. Especially beautiful gardens and pool with an island. All rooms have balconies and a view of the ocean.

Malibu. Costera Miguel Aleman No. 20, tel. 4–10–70; 80 rooms with balconies. A good secret to know. The nicest small hotel on the Costera. Time sharing operation. Rents rooms owners are not using; good value.

Maralisa. Avenida Enrique el Esclavo, Box 721; tel. 4–09–76; 90 rooms on the beach, three pools. Shuttle buses will take you up the hill. Seaside dining room. Sister hotel to the Villa Vera. A little jewel.

La Palapa. Fragata Yucatan No. 210, tel. 4–53–63, U.S. reservations (602) 957–4200; 400 rooms. All rooms are small suites with ocean view, and kitchenettes. Location on the ocean in a quiet residential section.

El Presidente. Box 933, Costera Miguel Aleman; tel. 4–17–00; U.S. (800) 228–3278. 422 rooms. Restaurants (the only kosher restaurant in town is open during the season) pools, tennis. The "action packed" part of The Strip begins here.

Moderate

Arbela. Costera Miguel Aleman No. 1270, opposite Golf Club; tel. 4–21–64. 50 rooms. Small and well located on the strip.

Boca Chica. Playa Caletilla; tel. 2–60–14; U.S. (800) 223–5695. 45 rooms. Five-story beautiful location across from Palao Restaurant. Quiet with magnificent view from every balcony. Walk down the hill to the beach or swim from hotel pier.

Casa Blanca. Cerro de la Pinzona; tel. 2–12–12, U.S. (800) 421–0767. 120 rooms. One of the early favorites high on the hill. Quiet and comfortable; spectacular view of the bay; a 5-minute ride to the beach.

Copacabana. Costera Miguel Aleman; U.S. tel. (305) 588–8541. Newest hotel on the beach, ½ block off the Costera. All 420 rooms have balconies with an ocean view.

Elcano. Costera Miguel Aleman and Box 430; tel. 4–19–50; 140 rooms with balconies. One of the golden oldies for those in the know. Quiet, well located charm, just off the Costera. One step to the beach.

Maris. Costera Miguel Aleman; tel. 5–84–40. 84 rooms. Another oldie but goodie.

El Mirador. Quebrada No. 74; tel. 2–45–64. 131 rooms. High on the hill; one of the first on the scene. The nightclub, La Perla, has the best view of the world famous divers.

Mozimba. Playa Langosta at the base of the hill to Coyuca 22; tel. 2–15–29. 30 rooms. Newly renovated by U.S. owners.

Romano's Le Club. Costera Miguel Aleman, corner Tikitiki Street; 300 rooms; tel. 4–77–30. Rococo seaside hotel, lots of groups.

Sands. Costera Miguel Aleman, corner Juan de la Cosa; tel. 4–22–60. 60 rooms; across from Acapulco Plaza and the beach. Small pool. Good value.

El Tropicano. Costera Miguel Aleman No. 510 across from Baby O; tel. 4–10–00; U.S. (800) 334–7234. 137 rooms. Pretty little hotel with all amenities. The beach is across the street.

Inexpensive

Auto-Ritz. Avenida Magallanes one half block off the Costera; tel. 5–80–23; U.S. (800) 458–6888; 103 rooms. Good value.

Belmar. Gran Via Tropical, corner Avenida de las Cumbres in Traditional Acapulco; tel. 3–80–98. A short walk down the hill to Caleta Beach. An old favorite with repeat visitors.

Los Flamingos. Avenida Lopez Mateos, Box 70; tel. 2–06–96. 47 rooms. High on a hill in a section that was the ultimate a few years ago. A five-minute ride from downtown and the beaches.

De Gante. Costera Miguel Aleman 265; tel. 5–02–32. 143 rooms. An old favorite across the street from Hornos Beach.

Vilia. Ave. Roqueta No. 54; tel. 3–33–11. 60 rooms. Chic, well maintained, this was once *the* place to stay. A short walk down the hill to the beach.

Condos and Villas

There are plenty of spectacular condominiums and villas to rent. Villa rates range from $150 to $600 (and up) per day depending on size, location, and services. One to three couples can share. Three-bedroom condos average $225 per day. *Ron Lavender/Bachur & Associates* can arrange it all. Tel: 5–71–51. You can also call *Sundominiums* (800) 547–6334; *Condoworld* (800) 521–2980; *Creative Leisure* (800) 227–4290 or MaryAnn Rivas, 4–36–60.

Trailer Parks

Playa Suave. Costera Miguel Aleman 739; tel. 5–33–16. Good location; all facilities. Reserve in advance.

Coloso. 5 miles out of town; all facilities.

IXTAPA/ZIHUATANEJO

Ixtapa/Zihuatanejo is a two-town, world-class resort that is well on its way to stardom.

If you looked at them on the map a few years ago, you might have said that it would never work. Two sprawling bays at the foot of the Sierra Madre Mountains—Palmar, which is now Ixtapa, and Zihuatanejo, then only a speck of a primitive fishing village, are separated by a jutting rock promontory called Punta Esteban. A dozen years ago, Ixtapa was nothing more than a stretch of palm lined virgin beach and Zihuatanejo was known only by a handful of residents and a few hearty travelers who enjoyed a rustic vacation lifestyle.

However, Fonatur, Mexico's National Trust Fund for Tourism Development, waved its magic wand, building connecting highways and roads, and completing an ultra modern infrastructure. Glittering hotels grew up along Palmar Bay, and international visitors began to discover the spectacular natural beauty that only a handful of hearty travelers had known before. In less than a dozen years, Ixtapa/Zihuatanejo grew into a dazzling duo. This knockout, two-for-the-price-of-one resort is attracting the attention of international travelers at a staggering rate. It delights the most sophisticated sun worshippers as well as those who truly like to get away from it all.

Though visitors might still have the feeling of being in a place that is on the threshold of development, all of the comforts and amenities that sophisticated travelers are accustomed to are present. An unspoiled, back to nature ambience prevails.

Even though Zihuatanejo has grown to a population of over 40,000, you have the feeling that it hasn't changed for centuries, and it plays a perfect counterpoint to Ixtapa's modernity. Perhaps nowhere in the world blends the past and the present so harmoniously.

Ixtapa/Zihuatanejo lies 150 km up the coast from Acapulco. It is an easy 3½-hour drive over a wide highway. Most of the area is sparsely populated and covered with lush tropical foliage. Small towns dot the highway and if you take the time to stop and explore off the main road, you're likely to discover some extraordinarily beautiful beaches. If you were to continue along the coast past Ixtapa, you would leave the state of Guerrero, (which is also home for Acapulco) and be in the state of Michoacán in about two hours.

The area's greatest assets are its natural beauty and the weather. Average year-round temperature is 78°F. It is slightly cooler than Acapulco. Ixtapa/Zihuatanejo is also less humid. June, July, and September are the rainiest months, but showers are usually short and many fall at night.

Dress is also slightly less formal than Acapulco. Men never need socks, ties or jackets. Ladies need a well-put-together look, but the costumes and glitz that one sees in Acapulco is not part of the scene here. Zihuatanejo is still less formal than Ixtapa. There you can get away with jeans or neat shorts and a cover up or tee shirt day and night.

A smooth, broad road links Playa Linda with the Hotel Zone. The Ixtapa Hotel Zone, a row of sparkling hotels, lines Palmar Bay. Paseo Ixtapa stretches through it past the golf club.

At the end, it turns off to Camino Real Hotel. A smaller road to the left of the entrance to Camino Real leads to a cluster of restaurants, including Villa de la Selva, Kon-Tiki, and the Ibiza disco. The main road continues winding around to Zihuatanejo. Just keep heading for the water. Turn right off the main highway and you'll reach downtown Zihuatanejo. Go straight and you'll reach a small turn off for La Ropa Beach.

Zihuatanejo is four miles (a 6–10 minute ride over a smooth highway) from Ixtapa. The Zihuatanejo International Airport which serves them both is 13 miles from the Hotel Zone.

A smooth, broad road links Playa Linda, the westernmost beach with the Hotel Zone.

Zihuatanejo is a bustling little cobblestone town that is thoroughly Mexican.

Zihuatanejo means "Place of the Women" in the Nahuatl Indian language. It was once occupied by the Cuitlalteca Indians who had a matriarchal society. In the post-conquest 1500s, it became an important port for Mexico's trade with the Orient. Today, it is a port-of-call for several cruise ships.

Whether you prefer a vacation lifestyle that is old or new, you're sure to enjoy it all.

PRACTICAL INFORMATION FOR
IXTAPA/ZIHUATANEJO

TELEPHONES. The area code for Ixtapa/Zihuatanejo is 743. The tax on international calls is over 50%. International long distance calls can be made from the Telephone Office at Ascencio and Galeana, 9 A.M.–2 P.M. and 4–7 P.M.

HOW TO GET THERE. By Air. *Aeromexico, Mexicana de Aviacion,* and *Western Airlines* operate direct flights from U.S. Gateways to Zihuatanejo International Airport. Aeromexico and Mexicana de Aviacion operate flights from Mexico City. Flying time is approximately 35 minutes.

By Car. There is a new road from Mexico City. Driving time is about 9 hours. Acapulco is 3 ½-hour (237 miles) drive away, over a good road. There are three Government Inspection stops.

By Bus. *Estrella de Oro* operates deluxe air-conditioned buses to Mexico City, Acapulco, and other points. The trip to Mexico City takes about 11 hours and costs about $8. To Acapulco, it takes 5 hours and cost $4. *Flecha Roja* costs less and takes a bit longer. Both terminals are in downtown Zihuatanejo. Get there a half hour early. You must reserve one day in advance either in person or by sending someone.

By Cruise Ship. Zihuatanejo is a port of call for *Princess* and *Royal Viking* lines.

HOW TO GET AROUND. By Car. Rental cars can be found in both Ixtapa and Zihuatenjo. Average daily rate for a medium-size automatic air-conditioned four-door car is $60–$70, including mileage. Jeeps or Safaris cost about $45 day. Parking is easy, except for downtown Zihuatanejo. In season, reserve well in advance, specify air-conditioned and automatic, and have your reservation's number ready.

Unless you plan to travel great distances or to visit remote beaches, taxis and buses are far less expensive. A taxi ride from the Hotel Zone to downtown Zihuatanejo costs approximately $1.50, to Playa la Ropa, $2.50. "Collective" taxis, which you share with others (look for the city seal on the side), can be flagged down. The fare to Zihuatanejo from the Hotel Zone is 50¢. Taxi fare to the airport is about $5. A Combi costs $3.

By Bus. Minibuses run between the hotels in the Hotel Zone to Zihuatanejo about every hour. Stops are clearly marked. The fare is about 75¢.

Bicycles and **pedicabs** with a fringe on top *(carachas)* that kids can drive can be rented in the parking lot in front of Dorado Pacifico Hotel. Bikes cost $1 per hour; carachas, $6. The rental tent is open 9 A.M.–8 P.M. daily.

SPECIAL EVENTS. *Deep Sea Fishing Tournament:* first week in December; the Semana de Guerrero, a week long series of special events, including a food fair, cock fights, etc., usually takes place in late March or early April.

USEFUL NUMBERS AND ADDRESSES. Airlines. *Aeromexico:* Hotel Krystal, Ixtapa, and Juan Alvarez No. 34, Zihuatanejo, tel. 4–20–18, tel. 4–29–39; *Mexicana de Aviacion;* Vincente Guerrero, corner Nicolas Bravo, Zihuatanejo, tel. 4–22–08; *Western Airlines:* International Airport, Zihuatanejo, tel. 4–33–26; *State Tourism Office:* Avenida del Pescador (Seaside Walk), Zihuatanejo, tel. 4–22–07; *Combi Airport Transportation,* tel. 4–21–70.

Taxi stand: tel. 4–20–80.

Money Exchange: Enturesa Travel Agency, Ixtapa Shopping Center. Be prepared to wait. They only change foreign currency from about 10 A.M. to noon.

Banks. Banking hours are 9 A.M.–1:30 P.M., Monday–Friday. *Bancomer,* La Puerta Shopping Mall, Ixtapa; *Bank of Mexico,* Nicolas Bravo 39A, Zihuatanejo; *Multibanco Comer Mex,* Vincente Guerrero, corner of Ramirez; *Banco Serfin,* Paseo Cocotal 22, Zihuatanejo.

Rent-a-Car offices are at the airport or: *Avis,* Hotel El Presidente, tel. 4–20–13; *Budget,* Dorado Pacifico, tel. 4–30–60; *Dollar,* Hotel Riviera del Sol, Ixtapa, tel. 4–24–06; *Hertz,* Paseo del Cocotal, Zihuatanejo, tel. 4–30–50 or 4–22–55, and Holiday Inn Hotel, Ixtapa, tel. 4–23–96; *National,* Hotel Krystal, Ixtapa, tel. 4–26–18, ext. 1110. Fast Jeeps: La Puerta Shopping Mall, tel. 4–27–78.

HOTELS. In general, the kind of big, modern hotels that travelers have become accustomed to finding in other Pacific resort areas are located in Ixtapa. Zihuatanejo hotels are smaller and cozier. A few of them meet international standards of sophistication. Unless mentioned otherwise, all hotels are European Plan. Categories in both cities are based on the same price ranges as in Acapulco.

Ixtapa

All hotels mentioned are located on Palmar Bay unless noted.

First Class

Camino Real. Creme de la creme. 450 air-conditioned rooms and suites. 6 suites have private pools. Every room has a servi bar, a spacious balcony with an ocean view, a patio, and a heavenly hammock. 7 bars and restaurants (La Esfera is tops), 4 pools, 4 tennis courts, watersports facilities, and shopping mall. No TV to spoil the reverie. Tel. 4–20–13; U.S. reservations (800) 228–3000.

Krystal. One of the most popular hotels on the strip. The town's top disco and restaurant are in the "front yard." 260 rooms and suites, all with individual air-conditioning control, ocean view, private terrace, and color TV. 5 bars and restaurants, pool with a waterfall, tennis courts, racket ball courts, and water sports. Airy lobby, beautiful public areas, tropical decor. Tel. 4–20–13; U.S. reservations (800) 231–9860.

Expensive

Club Mediterranee. Playa Quieta; 375 air-conditioned rooms, all sports facilities, pool, dining room, theater/nightclub. All rooms are part of week-long packages. Tel. 4–20–13; U.S. reservations (800) 528–3100.

Dorado Pacifico. 285 air-conditioned rooms, all facing the beach. Pool, children's pool, two tennis courts, 5 bars and restaurants. Shining glass, wood, and stucco decor. Tel. 4–30–60; Telex: 01773655.

Ixtapa Sheraton. 381 air-conditioned rooms and suites in two towers. All have ocean or mountain view, climate control, FM radio, and refrigerator/bar. Towering atrium lobby with inside glass elevator, 5 bars and restaurants, pool, wading pool for children, water sports. Tel. 4–31–84; U.S. reservations (800) 325–3535.

El Presidente. 440 air-conditioned rooms, 2 restaurants, 2 bars, a pool and tennis courts. Charming Mexican colonial style ambience. Outside glass elevator. Tel. 4–20–13; U.S. reservations (800) 854–2026.

Riviera del Sol. 500 air-conditioned rooms with ocean view; 2 pools, 4 restaurants, 3 bars, a disco; tennis courts and water sports. Tel. 4–24–06; U.S. reservations (800) 223–9868.

Moderate

Castel Palmar. 110 air-conditioned rooms with individual climate control. Pool, 2 bars, two restaurants, two tennis courts, playground; ideal for families. Tel. 4–23–41; U.S. reservations (800) 854–2026.

Holiday Inn. 238 air-conditioned rooms with ocean view; pool tennis court, water sports, 2 restaurants. Mexican and continental cuisine; disco. Tel. 4–23–96; U.S. reservations (800) 238–8000.

Inexpensive

Playa Linda. Playa Quieta. Rock bottom prices. 250 dormitory type rooms that accommodate 1–4 people. Tents can also be rented. There is a fully equipped trailer park with restaurants, bar, sports, and cooking facilities.

Note: Three new hotels are scheduled to open in 1987: **Aquamarina,** a 150-room hotel on the bay; **Los Aves,** a 120-room hotel behind Ixpamar Mall, and **Puertas del Mar,** a condo-hotel nearby. The **Aristos** may reopen as well.

Zihuatanejo

Zihuatanejo has a number of small hotels. Most are cozy and have a faithful clientele of repeat visitors, and almost all are within easy walking distance of town and a beach. If you want a room during Christmas or Easter weeks, reserve a year in advance. Average room price here is $50 and below. Some rooms are $8–$10 if you settle for no frills.

First Class

Villa del Sol. Playa La Ropa. Apartado Postal No. 84, tel. 4–22–39. 17 rooms, most are stylish duplexes with tropical flair. A chic place with a pretty seaside bar/restaurant and the air of an international private club. Water sports and tennis court available. This is a jewel. Some guests reserve a year in advance.

Expensive

Fiesta Mexicana, a new hotel on Playa La Ropa, had 32 out of 120 rooms completed and operating at press time.

Sotavento. Box 2, tel. 4–20–32. Overlooking Playa La Ropa. 70 rooms high on a hill overlooking the bay. This was one of the area's first and best. Breezy open air lobby and nostalgic style. Big, fan-cooled or air-conditioned rooms, hammocks, two bars, seaside restaurant, room phones.

Villas Miramar. Tel. 91–743. Madera Beach. 12 beautiful new suites five minutes from downtown. Colonial style architecture, pool, restaurant. One of the prettiest new places on the scene.

Moderate

Bungalos Allec. Madera Beach. Six fan-cooled bungalows plus a restaurant. Tel. 4–21–42.

Bungalos Pacificos. Cerro de la Madera, tel. 4–21–12. Six small houses with view of the ocean.

Bungalos Urracas. La Ropa Beach, tel. 4–20–49. 10 bungalows with kitchens.

Catalina. Box 2, tel. 4–21–37. La Ropa Beach. 30 fan-cooled rooms overlooking the ocean. Elevator from the beach.

Hotel Avila. Juan Alvarez #8, tel. 4–20–10. 30 air-conditioned rooms with bath, restaurant.

Irma. Box 4, tel. 4–21–05, U.S. (212) 957–7730. Madera Beach. 75 fan-cooled rooms overlooking the bay. 2 pools, beach club restaurant, disco, beautiful terrace. This is an old favorite.

Posada Caracol. Box 20, tel. 4–20–35. Madera Beach. 60 air-conditioned or fan-cooled rooms, open-air disco, 2 pools, 3 restaurants, Chololo disco, water sports. Colonial decor.

Hotel Zihuatanejo. Pedro Ascencio 48, tel. 4–26–69. 45 fan-cooled rooms; downtown.

Inexpensive

Raul Tres Marias. La Noria #4, tel. 4–21–91. 24 fan-cooled units. Small hotel for local businessmen.

TOURS. Major hotels have travel agencies. If yours does not, try *Turismo Caleta* (tel. 4–24–91) in La Puerta Shopping Mall or *Paseos Ixtapa* in the Sheraton lobby (tel. 4–35–50, ext. 2070); *Ixtamar* in the Dorado Pacifico (tel. 4–28–81) or *American Express* in Hotel Riviera del Sol (tel. 4–34–05).

Zihuatanejo City Tour. This includes major points of interest in Zihuatanejo and is a good way to get oriented. It costs about $7 U.S.

Ixtapa Island. A 15-minute boat ride from Playa Quieta or a 45-minute ride from Zihuatanejo. If you go on your own, the fare is $1 round trip from Playa Quieta; $3 from Zihuatanejo. An excursion costs approximately $10–$12 U.S.

Tequila Catamaran. You can sail away from La Ropa Beach at 11 A.M. and 3 P.M. for three-hour cruises of the bay with stops for swimming and snorkeling. Tel. 4–25–30.

Playa Las Gatas. A pretty beach, accessible only by water, where you can enjoy swimming, snorkeling, and diving. A few small restaurants offer simple meals. An excursion costs about $10–$12. If you want to go on your own, ferry boats leave about every 15 minutes from Zihuatanejo dock. Round-trip fare is about $1.

SPORTS. Name your favorite tropical sport and chances are that you can find it.

Parachute rides can be arranged on hotel zone beaches in Ixtapa. A 12-minute ride costs about $5–$6.

Waterskiing, snorkeling, diving, windsurfing, and **sailing** can be arranged in the Ixtapa hotel zone or La Ropa beaches. Waterskiing costs about $20 an hour.

Tennis. Most major hotels in Ixtapa have tennis courts. The Palma Real Golf & Tennis Club also has courts lit for night play. Tennis is $5 an hour for day play; $7 for night play.

Deep Sea Fishing boats can be rented on the Municipal Beach at Zihuatanejo Pier and at Playa Quieta in Ixtapa. Rates range from $100–$250/day, depending on the size of the boat. Hotel travel agencies can usually arrange excursions, too. Prices includes tackle, bait, and a light lunch.

Windsurfing. Windsurfers can be rented on Las Gatas and La Ropa beaches as well as at Las Cuatas Beach Club; Cost about $9 an hour; $18 with lessons.

Golf. You can play it at the *Palma Real Golf & Tennis Club* at the end of the Ixtapa hotel zone. There is a par 72, 18-hole championship course, a pool, a restaurant, a snack bar, and a pro shop. Greens fees are about $18. Golf carts cost about $12. Golf and tennis equipment can be bought or rented at the clubhouse. Golf club rental, $7. Lessons are available. Tel. 4–22–80.

Scuba Diving. *Carlos* operates day and night diving excursions on Las Gatas Beach. *Oliverio* operates diving excursions on Ixtapa Island. A one-hour dive costs about $20–$25. *Casa Del Mar* offers 4-hour diving excursions from Zihuatanejo to Barra de Potosi for $20. Price includes lunch and two tanks. Tel: 4–21–19.

Snorkeling. *Salomon Bustos,* next to Sirena Gorda Restaurant in Zihuatanejo, operates four-hour snorkeling excursions to Playa Manzanillo for about $10. The price includes lunch.

 BEACHES. The Ixtapa/Zihuatanejo coastline is scalloped and winds around hills and cliffs forming a number of beautiful coves and inlets where conditions are ideal for sunning and swimming. Generally, these beaches are less populated, more unspoiled, longer, and broader than beaches in other leading resorts. Some are more easily reached by car, and some are accessible only by water. You can find a beach to fit your particular preferences, no matter what they are.

Playa Linda. This beach north of Playa Quieta has facilities for campers, mobile homes, and all RVs. Full facilities, bathrooms, rooms and cooking facilities are available. There is a pool and a playground. Horses can be rented.

Playa Quieta is just 5 minutes away on the scenic highway. Club Mediterranee is here, but the beach is public. The clear waters and lush vegetation are famous.

Playa Las Cuatas has a moon-shaped "bay" bordered by craggy rocks. Windsurfers, Hobie Cats and snorkeling equipment can be rented. There are reasonably priced classes in practically everything. Waterskiing boats are also available. Snacks are available 11:30 A.M.–4:30 P.M.

Palmar, the hotel zone beach, is 2.5 miles of seaside charm. It combines spectacular beauty with all facilities for ultra modern comfort, just a few steps from your door. This is one of the few beaches in the country that you can enjoy at night.

Playa Hermosa at the near end of Playa Palmar is the beautiful beach for the Camino Real Hotel. Towering, picturesque rock formations provide scenic contrast to the curved beach.

Ixtapa Island, a 15–20 minute boat ride from Playa Quieta (where Club Med is), is a nature preserve that provides a perfect getaway for scuba divers and those who enjoy uninterrupted sun worshiping in primitive surroundings. When you get off the boat, take the five-minute walk to the other side of the island, which has small restaurants, fine sand, and clear waters. Unfortunately, vendors have arrived.

Zihuatanejo

Municipal Beach. It curves around Zihuatanejo Bay and is a few steps from the downtown shopping and restaurant area. It is lined with cozy hotels and restaurants. Fishing trips and excursions to Ixtapa Island and Las Gatas Beach can be arranged at the pier.

Maderas Beach. Primitive and tiny with gentle waves, it is within easy walking distance of the Municipal Beach. Guests of hotels and bungalows tend to use this one. There are a few restaurants, but you can climb up to hotel dining rooms for lunch.

La Ropa is a bit farther out of town. Several small bungalows line it. Rustic, open-air restaurants frequented by locals and visitors alike dot its edge. Waves are gentle and swimming conditions are ideal. Equipment for water sports can be rented.

Las Gatas. Hearty hikers can walk here from La Ropa Beach in about 20 minutes, but those who want to avoid having to climb sharp rocks take the easy way and come by boat from Playa Quieta or the Municipal Pier. The legend goes that a Tarascan Indian king had a coral reef built so that his daughter could swim safely here. The reef plus warm, crystal clear waters make Las Gatas especially ideal for diving and snorkeling. Instructors are available for both. Miniscule restaurants line the beach beside the pier. **Arnoldo's** is good. Go farther down the beach if you want to get away from the crowds. The knockout white stucco house belongs to a famous Mexican race car driver.

SHOPPING

Ixtapa

Ixtapa is becoming one of Mexico's best resorts for shopping. Repeat visitors are amazed at the number of new malls, shops, and boutiques that spring up every season. Handicrafts and resort wear are the most popular items. Store hours are generally: 9 or 10 A.M.–1 or 2 P.M. and 4 or 5 P.M.–8 or 9 P.M.

Most hotels have a few shops. Camino Real's minimall is the best.

La Puerta, first mall on the scene, across from El Presidente Hotel, has a collection of good boutiques. *Mandarina,* and *La Gaviota* have nice selections of resort wear and accessories. *Bazaar La Guadalupana* may have more souvenirs per square inch than any other shop in the world.

Three other exciting new malls are right beside it—terracotta-colored *Ixpamar* and *Los Patios* and bright white *Los Fuentes. El Amanecer,* an excellent folk art shop with a fine collection, and *Soqui* for clothing are among the best in Ixpamar. *Luisa Conti* for original jewelry and *Chiquita Banana* and *Maroc* for decorative items in Los Patios are also tops. *Acapulco Joe, Wanda Amiero,* and *Polo* are in Los Fuentes. *Fiorucci* is in its own building. *Fernando Huertas,* which has well-selected fashions and folk art, and *Off Shore* are in Ixtapa Mall acros the way. *Under the Volcano,* in front of Mandiles Restaurant, is also good for folk art and resort wear.

Zihuatanejo

Downtown Zihuatanejo is also full of inviting shops and boutiques. However, most are small and the best merchandise is often not on display, so it's better to go in and try on. Dedicated shoppers will find their own favorites and get plenty of good buys. Indians display handicrafts in a street market on Juan Alvarez. Take time to bargain. Their asking prices are high.

La Danza, the folk art store behind the museum, is tops. The state handicrafts store on Paseo Cocotal is of little interest.

RESTAURANTS

Ixtapa

Dining out in Ixtapa is pleasant. You can pick a place to suit your mood and probably it will be within easy walking distance. Hotel dining rooms are generally good and many are air-conditioned. Try restaurants at hotels other than your own. Men never need jackets or ties and any well put together look is suitable for ladies. Some hotels hold special events such as Mexican fiestas or beach barbecues on different nights and generally anynoe is invited. An average dinner costs $15–$25. *Diners Club, Carte Blanche,* and *American Express* credit cards are often not accepted.

The La Puerta shopping mall has three restaurants: **Da Baffone.** Air-conditioned and open-air sections. Open for lunch and dinner; Italian specialties; tel. 4–23–15. **Itzel.** Open air, for lunch and dinner. Spareribs, steaks and seafood are the specialties. **La Hacienda.** Air-conditioned and open-air sections. Open for breakfast, lunch, and dinner. Seafood and steaks, plus Mexican dishes; tel. 4–22–11.

Villa Sakura. Next to La Puerta shopping mall. Air-conditioned; authentic Japanese garden and cuisine; dinner only; 6 P.M.–1 A.M.; tel. 4–36–00 or 4–37–06.

Villa de la Selva. Punta Ixtapa, up the hill from entrance to Camino Real Hotel. Picture perfect, knockout decor; stay from sunset through dinner. Seafood and meat specialties; reservations are advised in season. Open 6–midnight; tel. 4–20–96.

Carlos 'N Charlies. Crazy Polynesian setting at the end of the beach beside Castel Palmar Hotel. Serves pork, seafood, and chicken. Open noon to 5 P.M. to midnight, except Tuesdays.

Le Montmartre. Across from Dorado Pacifico. Offers authentic French food in a lovely, refined atmosphere upstairs overlooking the boulevard. Open for breakfast (8 A.M.–noon) and dinner (6 P.M.–1 A.M.).

Several new restaurants will be located in the new shopping malls. **Don Quixote** is already serving steaks and seafood. Paella is their specialty. Open 1 P.M.–midnight. **Pizza Ragazzi** is next door.

Los Mandiles serves food with a Mexican flavor in a colonial setting with contemporary touches. Lively live music from Veracruz begins at 8 P.M. Open 4:30–11:30 P.M.

Bogart's, beside Hotel Krystal, is an opulent, ultraromantic Moorish-style restaurant that recalls Casablanca, offers sophisticated dining and continental cuisine in an outrageous out-of-this-world setting. Open for dinner only; Tel. 4–26–18. It's a knockout!

Zihuantanejo

Downtown Zihuantanejo is packed with informal, picturesque places to dine. You'll discover them as you stroll. Many are cash only, so come prepared. Here are a few of the favorites.

La Bocana, Juan Alvarez No. 13, has great fresh seafood specialties. The atmosphere is lively and friendly. This is an up-to-date, solid old favorite. Good food. Good portions. Open 8 A.M.–11 P.M. Tel. 4–35–45.

Canaima. Paseo del Pescador, Playa Municipal and Cinco de Mayo. Zihua's first, overlooking the town beach and harbor. Rustic, open air dining; hearty food, fresh clams, and lobster specialties. Reserve for dinner; tel. 4–20–03.

El Castillo. Calle Ejido No. 25. It looks like a corner castle. Friendly bar, international meat and seafood specialties; beautiful table settings; divine desserts. Reserve; tel. 4–34–19.

Chili's, hidden away at No. 46 Ignacio Altamirano, serves Mexican specialties in a pleasant Mexican atmosphere. Tel. 4–37–67.

Coconuts. Avenida Agustin Ramierez No. 1. Friendly bar and garden restaurants in one of Zihuatanejo's oldest historical buildings. Scrumptious pies and pastries are prepared on the premises. Everybody loves it. Reservations advisable; tel. 4–25–18.

Garrobos. In the Tres Marias Hotel on Juan Alvarez. Popular place for paella and brochettes. Tel. 4–29–77.

La Gaviota, on Playa La Ropa, is a mini beach club with a dozen or so tables. It's popular with locals and visitors. **El Marlin,** next door, takes the overflow.

Gitano's. Nicolas Bravo, corner Cinco de Mayo. The seafood comes straight off the fishing boats which tie up at the pier a few yards away. Some meat dishes also available. Tel. 4–23–18.

La Margarita on Cinco de Mayo, a new place has great food in a cool, cozy setting. Tel: 4–35–55.

La Mesa del Capitan. Nicolas Bravo No. 18. One of the first. Two floors plus garden dining area; continental cuisine. Tel. 4–20–27.

Mi Casita, Calle Ejido No. 7, is clean, yummy, and friendly; 8 A.M.–11 P.M. You can watch the cook prepare your meal. Surf & turf, Mexican dishes, etc. at reasonable prices.

Nueva Zealanda, Cuauhtemoc 23. Popular soda fountain and cafeteria. Light, good meals and some of the best *licuados* (fruit and milk shakes) in town. Open 8 A.M.–11 P.M. Everybody goes here.

Orient Express, a sushi bar beside the entrance to Coconuts, is where you can watch the crowd go by.

Puntarenas. Across the bridge on the end of Juan Alvarez Street. Home cooked authentic Mexican food in a no-nonsense setting. Breakfast and lunch; no reservations; prepare to wait. This is a favorite with local and visitors in the know. Only open December 15–Easter.

El Sombrero, Paseo Cocotal. A local "in" place. Open for dinner. Simple, good, and popular.

A cluster of restaurants have popped up around Ibiza disco, offering dining with a panoramic view of the bay. **The Bay Club** is in a romantic setting overlooking the beach. Candlelight and occasional live music. A comfortable bar is downstairs. Open 5 P.M.–11 P.M. Tel. 4-38-44. **Kon Tiki,** next door, also overlooks La Ropa and offers happy hour 5–8 P.M. for those who like to watch the sunset. Open 1 P.M.–midnight. Tel: 4-24-71. **La Costa Look,** across the way, has a great view and serves light meals from 1 P.M.–1 A.M.

NIGHTLIFE. Though Ixtapa/Zihuatanejo appears to be a nature oriented early-to-bed destination, you can switch into high gear after dinner and find plenty of action and fun that lasts as long as you let it. Ixtapa hotels often feature shows with big name entertainment. Watch for signs around town.

Discos. Ixtapa's disco scene is booming. Entry fees are approximately $8–$10 per person. Drinks range from about $1 for a coke to $4 for imported whiskey and soda. *Christine's,* in front of the Hotel Krystal, is as classy and sassy as they come. Three video screens, smoke, lights, balloons, and other gimmicks make already lively evenings livelier. Open 10:30 P.M.–4 A.M. *Joy,* across the street, is also new and glittering. Comfortable tiers of tables let you watch the action on the dance floor when you're not helping to make it. Open 10:30 P.M.–5 A.M. *La Esfera* in the Camino Real Hotel, is also sleek and lively. Backgammon tables and a comfortable bar are just outside. This is another favorite with locals and visitors. Open 10 P.M.–4 A.M. *Ibiza* is a tiny place with small windows overlooking the ocean on the road to La Ropa. The Zihuatanejo crowd loves it.

FOOD AND DRINK

From Fiery to Subtle

by
MARGARET MEDINA

Margaret Medina lived in Mexico for 16 years. An Iowa State University graduate, and food consultant to several major U.S. corporations, she is a former art critic and for several years wrote all foods material in the Mexican edition of Reader's Digest.

Mexican cuisine is one of the world's most exciting kinds of cookery. It is also one of the most difficult to eat, not just because of its unique blend of fire, fat and fancy, but also because—unless you happen to be a Mexican, living in Mexico and part of a Mexican family with a vast and ancient cooking tradition—it is exceedingly difficult to find. Even in Mexico City, with its eight million inhabitants and two or three thousand restaurants, really superb Mexican cooking is the exception rather than the rule. In provincial cities and towns, where almost everybody goes home for dinner at midday and restaurants exist for tourists and the homeless few, food tends to be simply something to eat and not something that makes you (the superb Mexican accolade) "lick your fingers." Outside of the country, so-called Mexican cooking—the tacos and chili con carne and hot tamales of the American Southwest or an occasional big city restaurant—bear somewhat the same uncomfortable resemblance to real Mexican cooking that a howling monkey bears to man.

This is not because the United States, a country with a growing gourmet focus and a genuine interest in things foreign and exotic, would not relish fine Mexican cooking, but simply because the cuisine depends not only on unique techniques but also on unique ingredients, most of which grow only in Mexico and have never been successfully exported.

The basic technique is grinding, done traditionally on a stone grinding slab called a *metate* or in a stone grinding bowl called a *molcajete.* To a great extent, mechanical mills have replaced the *metate:* shortly after dawn, almost anywhere in the country, you can see lines of women and children carrying buckets of soaked corn ready to be ground into dough. To nearly as great an extent, the electric blender has replaced the *molcajete:* all the intricate sauces of fresh or dried chilis ground with herbs, spices, nuts, vegetables, fruits and sometimes chocolate, can be whirred together in a few moments with this appliance that is more popular in Mexico than in any other country in the world—and with good reason. Thanks to it, and to the neighborhood mill for grinding *masa,* Mexican women have at last gotten off their knees after thousands of years during which the most time-consuming activity of every day was the grinding of food. If you are served somewhat paperlike tortillas, it could be that the cob was ground with the corn to make the *masa*—an unfortunate way to economize.

What gets ground, however, has changed not a bit: corn is still the base and backbone of the Mexican diet. Almost all corn cookery starts by soaking the dried kernels in lime water to soften them, after which they are ground into a dough called masa. Some varieties of corn are simply soaked, peeled and boiled to make a number of different hominy soups all called *pozole.* Masa is the dough from which tortillas are patted or pressed and then baked on a clay or metal griddle, but *masa* can also be diluted with water and boiled to make a thickened beverage called *atole,* or it can be beaten with lard and leavening to make the fluffy dough for tamales (steam cooked with goodies inside), or it can be flavored or enriched with other ingredients and used to make a host of different snacks.

The second most important food in the Mexican diet is chili, which adds vitamins to the diet and flavor to bland tortillas. At least 80 different commonly-eaten chilies run the gamut from pea-sized to pear-sized, and come fresh in shades of green, yellow, orange and red, or dried in tones of red, brown and black. In flavor, chilies vary enormously: they can blister not only your tongue but any part of your lips they touch in passing, or they can be fresh and mild, warm and aromatic, sweet and spicy or smoky and rich. Be careful of the chili habañero, especially popular in the Yucatan.

Nearly as important are tomatoes: Mexico has the reddest, roundest, ripest tomatoes in the world, and exports them in large quantities, but it also has a tiny green wild tomato that grows inside a papery husk like a Japanese lantern, of which it exports very few, and those only in cans.

Other foods which were gifts from Mexico to the Old World include avocados, chocolate, peanuts, squash, beans, vanilla, turkey and many tropical fruits, all of which have enormous importance in Mexican cookery, as do numerous herbs, vegetables and fruits which still grow only in this country.

In return for what Mexico contributed to world cookery, this country's cuisine has absorbed foods and influences from many lands. Such Spanish imports as onion, garlic, sugar, beef, pork, chicken and cheese have become wholly identified with Mexican cooking, and later invaders added further riches not the least of which is bread. The crisp-crusted French roll, as delicious in Mexico as in its native land, is nearly as popular as the tortilla, and so are the endless number of sweet rolls. Here Mexican artistry has worked the same extraordinary variations on bread that Mexican artisans worked on imported Spanish architectural forms. The Germans contributed a deft touch to sausage-making and honey production, but their greatest contribution is a liquid asset: Mexico's beer, from such light ale-types as Bohemia, Superior, Yucatan's Carta Clara or XXX Clara ("Tres Equis Clara") to heady dark bock-types such as XX ("Dos Equis") and Nochebuena, is rightly world-famous. Italy's pasta has become a daily staple in most Mexican homes. And American hamburgers, hotcakes, pies and doughnuts are still making inroads.

Real Mexican Cooking Rare

It is strange but true that you can find almost any of these imported cuisines in Mexico City, and even Guadalajara and Monterrey and other big cities, more easily than you can find really well-prepared Mexican cooking. Traditional Mexican foods are laborious and time-consuming to make, but that isn't the real reason why restaurants feature "international" cooking. After decades of dealing with flocks of tourists, Mexican restaurant and hotel owners have come to the conclusion that most people want to eat what they're used to eating. If a lavish *mole,* lovingly blended and slowly simmered, is going to produce shrieks of dismay, it's better to offer roast beef and be done with it.

A few Mexican specialties have proved to be popular with almost all tourists, so many good restaurants do feature *carne asada,* which is a thin strip of beef fillet quickly broiled and served with fried beans, sauteed strips of hot green pepper, the rich avocado sauce called *guacamole,* and perhaps other garnishes such as an enchilada or two.

Or you can find *tacos de pollo,* which will surprise you if you are used to California "tacos," and will delight you whether or not you've ever heard the word before. Usually, such tacos are tortillas rolled into tubes around a filling of shredded chicken, fried until crisp, and served with guacamole, a spoonful of heavy sour cream, fried beans, and assorted garnishes such as radishes and onions.

In reality, this is only one special version of the taco, for in Mexico, anything rolled up in a tortilla is a taco, and the tacos sold from street stands (rarely to be recommended to any traveler) are neither fried nor garnished. The Hotel Camino Real in Mexico City offers appetizer-sized tacos with assorted fillings, a fine snack to go with drinks before dinner. But two restaurants in the capital make a real specialty of Mexican food at its best, beautifully served in a charming environment. One is the Fonda El Refugio, at Liverpool 166; the other is the Restaurant Jardín del Angel, at Florencia 32. Both are in the Pink Zone and easy to get to from any hotel. Less elegant, less costly and also delightful is the Círculo del Sureste, at Lucerna 12, which serves better Yucatecan food than you're likely to find in Yucatán. And, for men only, a fine place to taste Mexican *antojitos* or snacks at their best is in men's bars, such as El León de Oro at Martí 101, which still features a continuous and abundant free lunch to keep you drinking.

But anyone who really wants to get acquainted with Mexican cooking will venture out into the provinces to discover the astonishing variations which can be played on a basic theme of corn, chili, tomatoes and beans. In this country, the traveling gourmet moves with a caution composed of equal parts of temptation, frustration and dread. Like many other countries, Mexico is full of stories about famous regional specialties, which turn out to be either impossible to find or else perfectly findable, but also tough, leathery, greasy, caustic, cathartic or at the least, perturbing. This perfectly normal picture of average highway cookery in many parts of the world is further complicated by that standard piece of tourist equipment in Mexico, fear of bugs.

Surely nothing in the world smells more enticing than a griddle full of *sopes,* which are little rimmed dishes of corn dough, fried and filled with beans and cheese and chile, and covered with shredded lettuce and fried spicy sausage and more cheese and chili. Fit that, if you can, into the cautious recommendation that you should eat "only cooked vegetables, fruits that can be peeled, no pork, no cheese and no chili" in Mexico.

Because so many tourists travel with this excessive caution, few hotels and tourist-oriented restaurants in the provinces offer much in the way of their region's special dishes. Restaurants catering to the local inhabitants usually do serve the regional specialties, and these are often found at their best in or around the town marketplace. If you are practical, realistic, self-disciplined and have eliminated both the gambler and the reckless hedonist in yourself, you will be able to walk through the marketplace filled with soft-boiled eggs and hard-boiled righteousness. If you are wholly mindless, you will succumb to the first seven tantalizing offerings placed in your path and immediately thereafter to at least five of the interesting variations on the normal functioning of the gastrointestinal system that abound in this land.

There are, on the other hand, hundreds of thousands of foreigners who have traveled through Mexico with open eyes, a lively curiosity and a real desire to taste and know a kind of cookery which has been called one of the ancient world's three original cuisines and the contemporary world's least known, with no misadventures whatsoever.

The rules for this kind of adventure are simple, composed mostly of moderation, respect and good judgment. Avoid any place which is not absolutely clean. When in doubt about the drinking water, choose

bottled beverages and drink them without ice, or select something
which has been boiled: coffee, tea, and any of the leaf—or flower—teas
which might be offered to you. *Café con leche* made with freshly boiled
milk is safe, almost always perfectly delicious, and a comforting way
to end a long day's journey. Experiment with tropical juices made fresh
to your order at many attractive small fruit stands, but avoid absolutely
the large jugs of prepared drinks you'll see in many places. In good city
restaurants that use purified water and ice, be sure to try these delicious
drinks of tamarind, jamaica flower, or lemonade speckled with tiny
seeds called *chía*. But don't risk them on the street.

Avoid, and with conviction, foods known to have considerable risk.
Unrefrigerated dairy products including fresh cheese, can cause too
much trouble to be worth playing about with, and so can lettuce (except
in top-quality restaurants), unrefrigerated protein foods, or uncovered
or unwrapped foods sold in the open, except for things prepared right
before your eyes.

But don't be startled by unusual wrapping. Steaming tamales
wrapped in corn husks are just as protected as anything covered with
cellophane, and so are the little bundles of *barbacoa* (mutton wrapped
in the parchment-like lining of maguey leaves) you may find in the State
of Mexico and other parts of the high central plateau. As your travels
take you into other regions of the Republic, you might, with a judicious
blend of zest and caution, pursue some of these famed specialties:

In the North

Mexican restaurants in the U.S. seem to be operated almost entirely
by former inhabitants of the Mexican states of Sonora and Chihuahua,
so at least some of the food you will find in these areas may be familiar
to you. Tamales tend to be fat and fully-stuffed, tacos look like turnovers, enchiladas are mostly red and filled with fine Cheddar-type
Chihuahua cheese and raw onion. Tortillas are frequently made from
wheat flour, and *burritos* are made from these tortillas, wrapped around
a filling of scrambled egg with beef jerky. Nice things are done with
beans in this part of the country—they may have cheese stirred into
them, or tomatoes and onions or *chorizo.* Chihuahua fattens fine beef,
makes great cheese and grows beautiful apples. Sonora is a clean and
beautiful state where good cooks prosper: try *chili con queso,* one of the
world's noble soups.

As you move toward the Gulf of Mexico, these same dishes continue
to be popular—jerky (called *machacado*), wheat tortillas and red chili
sauces. Coahuila is a grape state, which means wine, and is also noted
for its pecan candies, rolls of caramel fudge covered with pecan halves,
cones of panocha studded with nuts, pralines. Broiled young kid, kid
simmered in a sinister-sounding but delicious blood sauce, and broiled
ribs of beef are specialties of *Nuevo León,* which also grows Mexico's
sweetest oranges. Tamaulipas, on the Gulf, adds the fine freshness of
seafood and tropical fruits to the hotly sauced foods of the arid North.
Most of the entire Northern desert country has some favorite way of
serving tripe in a thick soup. Names vary: you may run into *birria,
menudo* or *café de hueso.* These dishes are hearty and delicious. San

Luis Potosí makes one of the best of them, and even better *quesadillas,* which are turnovers made of stuffed corn dough. But this state's real fame comes from its cactus fruit, which is made into a fermented drink, into flat little cakes called *queso de tuna,* and into a lovely sticky preserve called *melcocha.*

Central and Coastal Mexico

Some states are best known for what they produce, such as Sinaloa and Nayarit, with their long Pacific coastline, fine shellfish, and many varieties of bananas. Mazatlán's seafood is superb, particularly the giant oysters that are at once tender and almost crisp, opened before your eyes in restaurants right on the beach.

The regions of greatest cooking fame in Mexico are Guadalajara and Puebla, with traditions that are heavily Colonial and as loaded with history as with ingredients. Puebla is the home of Mexico's national dish, mole, with its 20 or 30 different spices, nuts, chilies, fruits and so forth. It also makes some strange and intriguing wild fruit liqueurs and a whole host of exciting things to eat, including *chalupas* and *sopes,* all laced with carefully blended sauces that carry a heady dash of cloves and cinnamon in a rich chile base. In Guadalajara, you should try Jalisco's *pozole,* which is a good antidote to Jalisco's tequila.

Veracruz does wonderful things with seafood—fish, shellfish and turtle, cooked in tomato sauces laced with sherry, almonds, raisins and capers. Even better are the freshly boiled shrimp, as pink as a baby's thumbnail, sold from baskets in the central plaza. At Boca del Río near Veracruz you can try all the abundance of Gulf seafood.

Across the country on the Pacific coast, Acapulco involves itself in "international" cooking and tends to be disappointing when it comes to fish, with the exception of *ceviche,* an entirely marvelous sort of eat-it-anytime made of raw fish "cooked" by marinating it in lime juice, and seasoned with a symphony of oil, orégano, onion, chile and tomato, plus olives, maybe, and avocado, almost always.

One fresh-water fish in Mexico is exceptional, and has brought gourmets from many parts of the world to sample it: this is the white fish of Lakes Pátzcuaro and Chapala. The raw fish is scaleless and nearly translucent; the cooked fish is unbelievably delicate in texture and flavor.

Move from Pátzcuaro to nearby Morelia and you're in the heart of candy land. Regional sweet specialties vary from old-fashioned chocolate ground on stone and seasoned with cinnamon or almonds to blocks and sheets of fruit pastes made from guavas, apples, strawberries or quinces, to sticky, creamy or chewy candies made of caramelized milk and sugar flavored with wine. Not too far away is Celaya, famed for its thick caramel sold in little boxes as well as in jugs and jars, but named for the boxes: *cajeta.* And a step further on is Irapuato, which exports tons of frozen strawberries but keeps a few for its local specialty, crystallized strawberries.

Southeast Mexico

Oaxaca, Chiapas and Yucatán are jungle country, and the cooking is different and delicious. Tamales are no longer rolled in corn leaves: you'll find square, flat little puddings wrapped in banana leaves, tasting marvelously of artichoke. Oaxaca's *mole* is black, milder than Puebla's, and at its best in the public market. Chiapas has mountains above its jungles and thus such high-country specialties as ham and a unique cheese the shape of a cannonball, good plain, and even better stuffed with a spicy meat filling. Yucatecan cooking is wholly unique, fragrant rather than hot, seasoned with *achiote* and the juice of sour Seville oranges mixed with garlic and black pepper. Look, especially, for *cochinita pibil,* which is suckling pig rubbed with these seasonings and slowly baked in a banana leaf wrapping.

You may be offered venison in Yucatán, Quintana Roo or Campeche, and you will almost surely be offered baby shark, called *cazón.* Never pass up an opportunity to try Moro crab in this area: it is unbelievably sweet and succulent.

Or you can avoid all these strange new foods and travel through Mexico subsisting happily on steak, eggs, fine bread and soups so universally excellent that you will rediscover the reason for eating soup, just as you can stay in the capital city and feast on Swiss fondues, French duck à l'orange, Italian osso bucco, German bratwurst, or American tunafish sandwiches. What you miss will be the unique flavor of a country with a cuisine truly its own, that mellows by a marriage of continents a taste as wild and raw as dripping jungles, parched deserts, and ancient pyramids against the sun.

MAP OF MEXICO

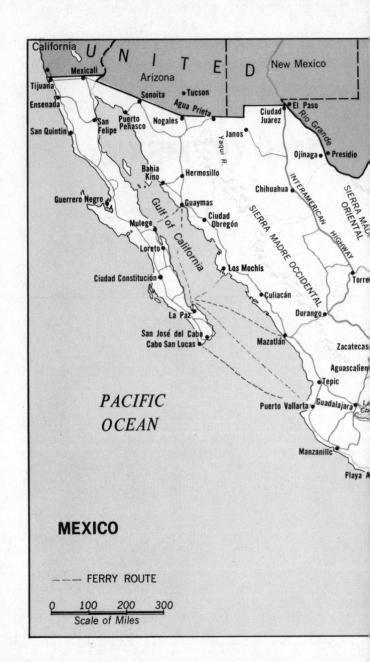

California
UNITED
Mexicali
Arizona
Tijuana
Sonoita
Tucson
New Mexico
Ensenada
Agua Prieta
San Quintin
San Felipe
Puerto Peñasco
Nogales
Janos
Ciudad Juarez
El Paso
Rio Grande
Presidio
Ojinaga
Bahia Kino
Hermosillo
Yaqui R.
Chihuahua
INTERAMERICAN HIGHWAY
SIERRA MADRE ORIENTAL
Guerrero Negro
Gulf of California
Guaymas
Mulege
Ciudad Obregón
SIERRA MADRE OCCIDENTAL
Loreto
Los Mochis
Ciudad Constitución
Culiacán
Torre
La Paz
Durango
San José del Cabo
Cabo San Lucas
Mazatlán
Zacatecas
Aguascalien
Tepic
PACIFIC OCEAN
Puerto Vallarta
Guadalajara
Manzanillc
Playa A

MEXICO

----- FERRY ROUTE

0   100   200   300
Scale of Miles

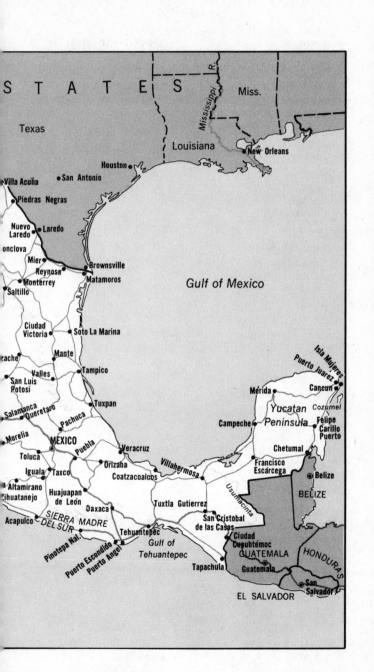

Index

FODOR'S TRAVEL GUIDES

Here is a complete list of Fodor's Travel Guides, available in current editions; most are also available in a British edition published by Hodder & Stoughton.

U.S. GUIDES

Alaska
American Cities (Great Travel Values)
Arizona including the Grand Canyon
Atlantic City & the New Jersey Shore
Boston
California
Cape Cod & the Islands of Martha's Vineyard & Nantucket
Carolinas & the Georgia Coast
Chesapeake
Chicago
Colorado
Dallas/Fort Worth
Disney World & the Orlando Area (Fun in)
Far West
Florida
Fort Worth (see Dallas)
Galveston (see Houston)
Georgia (see Carolinas)
Grand Canyon (see Arizona)
Greater Miami & the Gold Coast
Hawaii
Hawaii (Great Travel Values)
Houston & Galveston
I-10: California to Florida
I-55: Chicago to New Orleans
I-75: Michigan to Florida
I-80: San Francisco to New York
I-95: Maine to Miami
Jamestown (see Williamsburg)
Las Vegas including Reno & Lake Tahoe (Fun in)
Los Angeles & Nearby Attractions
Martha's Vineyard (see Cape Cod)
Maui (Fun in)
Nantucket (see Cape Cod)
New England
New Jersey (see Atlantic City)
New Mexico
New Orleans
New Orleans (Fun in)
New York City
New York City (Fun in)
New York State
Orlando (see Disney World)
Pacific North Coast
Philadelphia
Reno (see Las Vegas)
Rockies
San Diego & Nearby Attractions
San Francisco (Fun in)
San Francisco plus Marin County & the Wine Country
The South
Texas
U.S.A.
Virgin Islands (U.S. & British)
Virginia
Waikiki (Fun in)
Washington, D.C.
Williamsburg, Jamestown & Yorktown

FOREIGN GUIDES

Acapulco (see Mexico City)
Acapulco (Fun in)
Amsterdam
Australia, New Zealand & the South Pacific
Austria
The Bahamas
The Bahamas (Fun in)
Barbados (Fun in)
Beijing, Guangzhou & Shanghai
Belgium & Luxembourg
Bermuda
Brazil
Britain (Great Travel Values)
Canada
Canada (Great Travel Values)
Canada's Maritime Provinces plus Newfoundland & Labrador
Cancún, Cozumel, Mérida & the Yucatán
Caribbean
Caribbean (Great Travel Values)
Central America
Copenhagen (see Stockholm)
Cozumel (see Cancún)
Eastern Europe
Egypt
Europe
Europe (Budget)
France
France (Great Travel Values)
Germany: East & West
Germany (Great Travel Values)
Great Britain
Greece
Guangzhou (see Beijing)
Helsinki (see Stockholm)
Holland
Hong Kong & Macau
Hungary
India, Nepal & Sri Lanka
Ireland
Israel
Italy
Italy (Great Travel Values)
Jamaica (Fun in)
Japan
Japan (Great Travel Values)
Jordan & the Holy Land
Kenya
Korea
Labrador (see Canada's Maritime Provinces)
Lisbon
Loire Valley
London
London (Fun in)
London (Great Travel Values)
Luxembourg (see Belgium)
Macau (see Hong Kong)
Madrid
Mazatlan (see Mexico's Baja)
Mexico
Mexico (Great Travel Values)
Mexico City & Acapulco
Mexico's Baja & Puerto Vallarta, Mazatlan, Manzanillo, Copper Canyon
Montreal (Fun in)
Munich
Nepal (see India)
New Zealand
Newfoundland (see Canada's Maritime Provinces)
1936 . . . on the Continent
North Africa
Oslo (see Stockholm)
Paris
Paris (Fun in)
People's Republic of China
Portugal
Province of Quebec
Puerto Vallarta (see Mexico's Baja)
Reykjavik (see Stockholm)
Rio (Fun in)
The Riviera (Fun on)
Rome
St. Martin/St. Maarten (Fun in)
Scandinavia
Scotland
Shanghai (see Beijing)
Singapore
South America
South Pacific
Southeast Asia
Soviet Union
Spain
Spain (Great Travel Values)
Sri Lanka (see India)
Stockholm, Copenhagen, Oslo, Helsinki & Reykjavik
Sweden
Switzerland
Sydney
Tokyo
Toronto
Turkey
Vienna
Yucatán (see Cancún)
Yugoslavia

SPECIAL-INTEREST GUIDES

Bed & Breakfast Guide: North America
Royalty Watching
Selected Hotels of Europe
Selected Resorts and Hotels of the U.S.
Ski Resorts of North America
Views to Dine by around the World

AVAILABLE AT YOUR LOCAL BOOKSTORE OR WRITE TO FODOR'S TRAVEL PUBLICATIONS, INC., 201 EAST 50th STREET, NEW YORK, NY 10022.